Thresholds
A "Complete" Table of the Borrowings in Yambo Ouologuem's *Le Devoir de violence*, and Why They Matter

Contemporary French and Francophone Cultures, 98

Contemporary French and Francophone Cultures

Series Editor

CHARLES FORSDICK
University of Liverpool

Editorial Board

TOM CONLEY
Harvard University

JACQUELINE DUTTON
University of Melbourne

LYNN A. HIGGINS
Dartmouth College

MIREILLE ROSELLO
University of Amsterdam

DEREK SCHILLING
Johns Hopkins University

This series aims to provide a forum for new research on modern and contemporary French and francophone cultures and writing. The books published in *Contemporary French and Francophone Cultures* reflect a wide variety of critical practices and theoretical approaches, in harmony with the intellectual, cultural and social developments which have taken place over the past few decades. All manifestations of contemporary French and francophone culture and expression are considered, including literature, cinema, popular culture, theory. The volumes in the series will participate in the wider debate on key aspects of contemporary culture.

Recent titles in the series:

84 Ari J. Blatt, *The Topographic Imaginary: Attending to Place in Contemporary French Photography*

85 Martin Munro and Eliana Văgălău, *Jean-Claude Charles: A Reader's Guide*

86 Jiewon Baek, *Fictional Labor: Ethics and Cultural Production in the Digital Economy*

87 Oana Panaïté, *Necrofiction and The Politics of Literary Memory*

88 Sonja Stojanovic, *Mind the Ghost: Thinking Memory and the Untimely through Contemporary Fiction in French*

89 Lucy Swanson, *The Zombie in Contemporary French Caribbean Fiction*

90 Lucille Cairns, *Eating Disorders in Contemporary French Women's Writing*

91 Sophie Fuggle, *France's Memorial Landscape: Views from Camp des Milles*

92 Clíona Hensey, *Reconstructive Memory Work: Trauma, Witnessing and the Imagination in Writing by Female Descendants of Harkis*

93 Christopher T. Bonner, *Cold War Negritude: Form and Alignment in French Caribbean Writing*

94 Akane Kawakami, *Michael Ferrier, Transnational Novelist*

95 Michael Gott and Thibaut Schilt, *Quebec Cinema in the 21st Century: Transcending the National*

96 Bruno Choaut, *Out of this World: Gnostic Encounters in Modern French Literature and Thought*

97 Ashwiny O. Kistnareddy, *Refugee Afterlives: Home, Hauntings, and Hunger*

CHRISTOPHER L. MILLER

Thresholds

A "Complete" Table of the Borrowings
in Yambo Ouologuem's
Le Devoir de violence, and
Why They Matter

LIVERPOOL UNIVERSITY PRESS

First published 2024 by
Liverpool University Press
4 Cambridge Street
Liverpool
L69 7ZU

Copyright © 2024 Christopher L. Miller

Christopher L. Miller has asserted the right to be identified as the author of this book in accordance with the Copyright, Designs and Patents Act 1988.

All rights reserved. No part of this book may be reproduced, stored in a retrieval system, or transmitted, in any form or by any means, electronic, mechanical, photocopying, recording, or otherwise, without the prior written permission of the publisher.

British Library Cataloguing-in-Publication data
A British Library CIP record is available

ISBN 978-1-83553-233-1 (hardback)
ISBN 978-1-83553-234-8 (paperback)

Typeset by Carnegie Book Production, Lancaster

For Christopher Rivers, always

Contents

Acknowledgments	ix

Part One

Chronology: Yambo Ouologuem and *Le Devoir de violence*	1

Part Two

Why the Borrowings Matter	9
Introduction	9
Can Words Be "Borrowed"?	13
Francophone Literary Borrowing and "Textual Ownership"	15
An Overview of the Borrowings in *Le Devoir de violence*	17
The Schwarz-Bart Connection, and a Comparison	21
Case Studies:	
1. Africanization	23
2. Textual Borrowing and Polyvocal History	27
3. Borrowing in/and Translation	41
Ouologuem's Forgotten Farewell: "The World Is False"	46
Conclusion	50
Notes	51

Part Three

The Borrowings in Yambo Ouologuem's *Le Devoir de violence*: A "Complete" Table	67
Index	III

Acknowledgments

I am grateful to Jean-Pierre Orban, Claire Riffard, and Guy Dugas for inviting me to present a draft of this work to their seminar "Manuscrits francophones: littératures du Sud, le processus de fabrication" on March 17, 2023, and to the participants in the discussion, especially Francine Kaufmann, Catherine Mazauric, Khalid Lyamlahy, and Elgas. Dominic Thomas was indispensable; Ben Smith, Manthia Diawara, Elian Peltier, Céline Gahungu, and Chérif Keïta were very helpful. Most of all, I am grateful to Joël Bertrand for his kind and generous collaboration. Deep gratitude to Christopher Rivers for editorial comments. I am indebted to the two anonymous readers for Liverpool University Press. I thank the staff and administration of Sterling Memorial Library at Yale for their incredible service before, during, and after the pandemic, without which this work would not have been possible. Chloe Johnson of Liverpool University Press has been a pleasure to work with, and I thank Sarah Davison of Carnegie Book Production for her production editing.

Translations from French are mine unless otherwise noted. A version of "Ouologuem's Forgotten Farewell" appeared in the journal *Continents manuscrits*, December 2023.

Publication of this book is made possible by the generous support of the Macmillan Center for International and Area Studies and the Henry Koerner Center for Emeritus Faculty at Yale.

PART ONE
Chronology
Yambo Ouologuem and *Le Devoir de violence*

1940
August 22: Birth of Yambo Amadou Ouologuem to a prominent family in Bandiagara, French Sudan, which became Mali at independence in 1960.

1962
Arrival of Yambo Ouologuem in France. He is admitted to the Lycée Henri IV, then to the Ecole Normale Supérieure; he earns an advanced degree in English, passes the *agrégation*, and teaches at a *lycée* in Charenton.

1963
Ouologuem submits his first manuscript to Editions du Seuil. It has nothing to do with Africa and is harshly rejected. It is entitled *Le Devoir de violence*.

1964
Ouologuem submits a second manuscript to Seuil, a collection of poems called *La Salive noire*. It is rejected. In December, he sends a third manuscript, a novel, *Humble soif*. It, too, is refused.
Ouologuem publishes "Marx et l'étrangeté d'un socialisme africain," in *Présence Africaine* 50, no. 2: 20–37.

1966
Ouologuem publishes "A Mon Mari" (To My Husband), in *Présence Africaine* 57, *Nouvelle somme de poésie du monde noir*, p. 95. The

2 Thresholds

poem is written from the point of view of an African woman married to an African man who is an eager assimilationist or *évolué*, leaving his wife feeling "under-developed" and "undernourished."

1967
October 11: After much negotiation and resistance from the publisher (discussed in this volume), Ouologuem signs a contract with Seuil for the publication of *Le Devoir de violence*, a novel about African history.

1968
July: *Le Devoir de violence* is printed, with a red band stating: "C'est le sort des Nègres d'avoir été baptisés dans le supplice" (It is the fate of the Blacks to have been baptized into suffering).

August 16: André Schwarz-Bart, the novelist and author of *Le Dernier des Justes* (Paris: Editions du Seuil, 1959, Prix Goncourt) who received a pre-publication copy of *Le Devoir de violence*, writes to François-Régis Bastide, editor of Seuil, in outrage about the similarities between his *Le Dernier des Justes* and *Le Devoir*. Mostly he is offended by Bastide's failure to let him know. At the same time he says, "Jamais livre n'en a gêné un autre" (One book has never stood in the way of another), and that he is flattered by Ouologuem's repurposing of his work. He never reproaches Ouologuem for the borrowings.

September: Publication of *Le Devoir de violence* by Editions du Seuil. At dates (not yet determined) during the fall, Seuil issues several slightly revised versions of the novel, apparently after learning of the borrowings from Schwarz-Bart's *Le Dernier des Justes*. This is only discovered in 2019, by Francine Kaufmann.

October 10: *Le Monde* publishes "Un Nègre à part entière" by Philippe Decraene, based on an interview with Ouologuem.

October 12: Matthieu Galey publishes "Un grand roman africain" in *Le Monde*.

November 18: *Le Devoir de violence* wins the Prix Renaudot. Thirty-six thousand more copies are printed; the total will exceed 100,000.

November 29: A law student writes to Seuil pointing out certain borrowings from Maupassant in *Le Devoir de violence*, calling it plagiarism.

At an unknown date in 1968, Ouologuem publishes a romance novel under the pseudonym Nelly Brigitta, *Le Secret des orchidées* (Paris: Editions du Dauphin, 1968).

Chronology 3

1969
Yambo Ouologuem publishes *Lettre à la France nègre* (Paris: Editions Nalis, 1968). The book is dated 1968 but appeared in 1969.
Ouologuem publishes an erotic novel under the pseudonym Utto Rodolph, *Les mille et une bibles du sexe* (Paris: Editions du Dauphin, 1969).
Ouologuem begins writing a novel titled *Les Pèlerins de Capharnaüm*, which is never completed nor published. Seventy-five typewritten pages are conserved at the Institut Mémoires de l'édition contemporaine (IMEC) archive. Jean-Pierre Orban describes the project as a "mythico-religious" narrative.

1970
Ouologuem publishes another romance novel as Nelly Brigitta, *Les Moissons de l'amour* (Paris: Editions du Dauphin, 1970).

1971
Release of the first English translation, by Ralph Manheim: *Bound to Violence*. In February and March, Ouologuem visits New York to promote the book. During his stay he signs a contract with Doubleday for five books and receives an advance of $30,000.
March 7: The *New York Times* publishes an interview with Ouologuem: Mel Watkins, "Talk with Ouologuem."
March 18: Ouologuem appears on *The Today Show*. His interview with Hugh Downs is briefly quoted by Thomas Hale in his book *Scribe, Griot, and Novelist* (Gainesville: University of Florida Press, 1990, p. 158), but no recording of the interview has been located.
Autumn: Eric Sellin publishes "Ouologuem's Blueprint for *Le Devoir de violence*," *Research in African Literatures* 2, no 2 (1971): 117–20. He discusses borrowings from Schwarz-Bart only, saying they were brought to his attention by a friend, Mohamed Saleh-Dembri (an Algerian politician). Sellin says he was dismayed and bewildered by the borrowings, but he never uses the word "plagiarism."
December 5: The *New York Times* lists *Bound to Violence*, the Manheim translation, as one of "Seven Books of Special Significance Published in 1971," along with John Updike's *Rabbit Redux* and a new edition of T. S. Eliot's *The Waste Land*. The unsigned article claims Ouologuem's novel to be "the first work by an African writer to have mastered and exploited both Western and African forms to create a major new

4   *Thresholds*

fiction ... Ouologuem commands changes of mood and idiom with dazzling assurance, shifting swiftly from animal sensuality to cold brutality or witty intellection."

1972

After treatment in a psychiatric hospital in France, Ouologuem begins to spend more and more time in Mali. He becomes a devout Muslim.

February 18: Ouologuem sues Seuil in a Paris court for non-payment of funds owed to him; the suit drags on until 1976.

May 5. The unsigned article "Something *New* Out of Africa?" is published in the *Times Literary Supplement* (*TLS*) reporting borrowings from Graham Greene's *It's a Battlefield*. The *New York Times* reports on this on the same day ("Novel Is Likened to Greene's Book: African's 'Bound to Violence' Held Similar to 'Battlefield.'"). The scandal erupts and is widely reported.

May 13: Guy Le Clec'h writes the first article to be published in France reporting the borrowings: "Ouologuem n'emprunte qu'aux riches," *Le Figaro*.

June 10: Ouologuem defends himself in *Le Figaro* ("Polémique: *Le Devoir de violence*") and files suit against the newspaper for libel; the suit goes nowhere. In his defense he claims for the first time that his original manuscript had quotation marks around the borrowed passages, quotation marks which were, he alleged, removed by the publisher. An original manuscript is never found.

Harcourt Brace Jovanovich (the owner of Heinemann Educational Books) proposes to destroy copies of *Bound to Violence* and, at the request of Graham Greene's American agent, withdraws the novel from sales. Harcourt settles with Seuil for the sum of $4,786.12 in damages, which Seuil then debits from Ouologuem's royalty account.

Publication of "*Bound to Violence*: A Case of Plagiarism" by Robert McDonald, in *Transition* 41 (1972): 64–68.

Ralph Manheim's translation, *Bound to Violence*, is a finalist for the National Book Award for Translation.

Many other articles, book chapters, and essays discuss the question of plagiarism in the next few years.

1973

Spring: Seth Wolitz, "L'art du plagiat, ou une brève defense de Ouologuem," *Research in African Literatures* 4, no. 1: 130–34.

Yambo Ouologuem, R. Pageard, and M. T. Demidoff, *Introduction aux lettres africaines* (Paris: Editions de l'Ecole).

1974
January 12: Ouologuem publishes "Le Monde est faux" in *Jeune Afrique*, 678/679: 68–70. This is his last known publication. The editors' remarks say it is "a fragment of a forthcoming work, *Le Monde est faux.*"

1978
Ouologuem returns to Mali definitively.

1982
Christine Chaulet-Achour completes her thesis: "Langue française et colonialisme en Algérie: de l'abécédaire à la production littéraire," Université de Paris III, 1982. This was at the time the most complete analysis of borrowings in *Le Devoir de violence.*
Seuil stops printing *Le Devoir de violence.*

1992
Ouologuem's daughter Awa (sometimes cited as Ava) takes control of her father's literary affairs.

1998
Christopher Wise publishes his account of having encountered Ouologuem (who had not been interviewed in 30 years and had gone to great lengths to avoid intrusive critics) in Mali in 1997. See "In Search of Yambo Ouologuem," *Research in African Literatures* 29, no. 2 (Summer 1998), reprinted in *Yambo Ouologuem: Postcolonial Writer, Islamic Militant*, ed. Christopher Wise (Boulder, CO: Lynne Rienner, 1999). An acquaintance is quoted as saying, "Yambo has not been himself lately" (205), and Wise states that "Ouologuem never saw our approach" (207); and "At no point was Ouologuem willing to discuss his writing" (209).

2003
Ouologuem is interviewed for a film, *Yambo Ouologuem: le Hogon du Yamé*, by Moussa Ouane. Very little screen time is given to Ouologuem himself speaking. His ex-wife, Adama Diallo, speaks at some length, and his daughter, Awa, appears briefly. See https://www.youtube.com/watch?app=desktop&v=3m03P7B7—I.

6   Thresholds

Le Serpent à Plumes reissues *Le Devoir de violence*, authorized by Ouologuem's daughter, Awa Ouologuem.
Bound to Violence is removed from Heinemann's African Writers Series.

2004
The Cameroonian writer Eugène Ebodé visits Ouologuem in Sévaré. He meets "a furious man, with a grey beard, hair in disorder, bare chested … irritable, but in excellent physical health." Ouologuem speaks of his literary career, his Prix Renaudot, and of "French betrayal." He tells his guest that he became a strict Muslim "pour les emmerder tous" (to piss them all off). See https://www.jeuneafrique.com/1250691/culture/le-jour-ou-eugene-ebode-a-rencontre-yambo-ouologuem/.

2009
Publication of *The Yambo Ouologuem Reader: The Duty of Violence, A Black Ghostwriter's Letter to France, and The Thousand and One Bibles of Sex*, ed. and trans. Christopher Wise (Trenton: Africa World Press). This is the second translation of *Le Devoir de violence*.
Antoine Marie Zacharie Habumukiza makes major new contributions to the study of the borrowings, including Flaubert, in "*Le Devoir de violence* de Yambo Ouologuem: une lecture intertextuelle," his MA thesis, Queen's University, 2009.

2014
Joël Bertrand launches his first website devoted to borrowings in *Le Devoir de violence*. See 2016.

2016
March 8: Joël Bertrand adds many new materials to his website devoted to borrowings in *Le Devoir de violence*. His work began with a DEA thesis, Université de Provence, 1984: "L'intertextualité dans *Le Devoir de violence*." See 2023.

2017
October 14: Death of Yambo Ouologuem in a hospital in Sévaré, Mali. Sarah Burnautzki publishes *Les Frontières racialisées de la littérature française: contrôle au faciès et stratégies de passage* (Paris: Honoré Champion, 2017). Burnautzki was the first researcher given access to the Ouologuem-Seuil papers stored at the IMEC archive in Normandy, with restrictions on reproduction.

Chronology 7

2018
Seuil republishes *Le Devoir de violence* with a new, unsigned "Note de l'éditeur."

2019
Jean-Pierre Orban publishes "Livre culte, livre maudit: histoire du *Devoir de violence* de Yambo Ouologuem," reporting in depth on, and reproducing documents from, Ouologuem's files with Editions du Seuil held at IMEC.
Francine Kaufmann discovers that there are variants among the different printings of *Le Devoir de violence* made in the fall of 1968, likely in reaction to the realization of borrowings from Schwarz-Bart. Her research on this continues.

2021
Mohamed Mbougar Sarr, a Senegalese writer, publishes his novel *La Plus secrète mémoire des hommes*, which contains a fictionalized retelling of Ouologuem's life; the novel is dedicated to Ouologuem. It wins the Prix Goncourt for 2021 and is translated into English by Lara Vergnaud as *The Most Secret Memory of Men* (New York: Other Press, 2023) in conjunction with the Other Press republication of the Manheim translation of *Bound to Violence*; see 2023. Sarr's novel reignites interest in Ouologuem.

2023
Joël Bertrand publishes "*Le Devoir de violence* comme collage" on his website, with his updated, unabridged table of borrowings. See https://joelbertrand.wordpress.com/bound-to-violence-as-a-collage/.
September 23: Other Press republishes the Manheim translation of *Bound to Violence*, edited and with an introduction by Chérif Keïta. Publicity for the book highlights "the racist plagiarism scandal that devastated its author."

2024
July 3 (announced in 2023): Penguin Classics plans to reissue the Manheim translation, *Bound to Violence*, with the Keïta introduction.

PART TWO
Why the Borrowings Matter

Vous pouvez lire dans tous les sens possibles et imaginables. A chaque lecture, l'histoire est différente, et les combinaisons infinies.

(You can read in all ways that are possible and imaginable. With each reading, the story is different, and the combinations infinite)

—Yambo Ouologuem, *Lettre à la France nègre*, 1968

Le monde est faux et marche sur le malentendu.

(The world is false and works by way of misunderstandings)

—Yambo Ouologuem, *Jeune Afrique*, 1974

Introduction

In the tumultuous year of 1968, a young Malian writer living in France published his first novel: *Le Devoir de violence*, which would go on to be translated as *Bound to Violence* in 1971.[1] Hailed by *Le Monde* as "a great African novel," "the first African novel worthy of the name," *Le Devoir de violence* set off a firestorm in African literary circles for its thoroughgoing attack on the dominant ideology of Negritude, which it mocked as "black romanticism."[2] Ouologuem did not endear himself to the African cultural establishment by saying things like this in the press: "They have cultivated a cheap kind of folklore, designed to warm the hearts of philistine Negrophiles without obligation or sanction." He was outraged by "the scandal of contemporary politics."[3] Léopold Sédar Senghor, the undisputed chairman of the board of Negritude, scolded: "One cannot make a positive work of art while at the same time denying

10   *Thresholds*

all one's ancestors."[4] Ouologuem, of course, had no intention of making "a positive work of art."

Ostensibly the story of the perverse and sadistic Saïf dynasty, rulers of an empire called Nakem, *Le Devoir de violence* was a multipronged attack on assumptions about African literature. African writers were expected to revere their past; but Ouologuem depicted only a violence to which Africans were apparently "bound." If, in the nineteenth century, the colonizers thought they were coming in to oppress people, the joke was on them: the Saïfs had been doing that for hundreds of years. The novel is divided into four parts, following a certain evolution of literature: an oral epic recounting genealogy ("La Légende des Saïfs"); a heroic tale ("L'Extase et l'agonie"); a novel within the novel, told in ten chapters ("La Nuit des géants"); and finally something resembling modern theater ("L'Aurore").[5] The style shifts radically multiple times, as Ouologuem *borrows* from an enormous variety of texts throughout the course of the novel.

Le Devoir de violence won the 1968 Prix Renaudot. Ouologuem became famous, even appearing on the American *Today Show* in 1971 to promote the English translation. But in May of 1972, the *TLS* published an anonymous accusation of plagiarism: passages of *Le Devoir de violence* closely resembled parts of Graham Greene's novel *It's a Battlefield.*[6] An uproar ensued; the novel was withdrawn and left out of print for decades; Ouologuem went home to Mali and quit literature. *Le Devoir de violence* has been one of the most debated African novels ever since. The discussion, I want to suggest, has lacked overall coherence and should be reoriented in light of recent discoveries, namely a radical expansion of the documented borrowings in the novel.

For decades, criticism of *Le Devoir de violence* (*Bound to Violence*) has been divided into two camps: the historical and the textual, with the latter largely devoted to the borrowings for which the novel is famous. Critics have behaved as if the two approaches were mutually exclusive. Christopher Wise writes disdainfully of "American critics" whose "antics" involving the borrowings are criticized by (unnamed) "African colleagues."[7] On the other side, have those focused on the borrowings neglected the historical dimensions of the novel? Perhaps. I hope to propose a remedy for this false opposition.

It is widely felt among some critics (African or other) that the borrowings are a sideshow; that attention to the borrowings detracts from the real work of the novel, which is a revolution in the way the African past is constructed and a thorough destruction of Negritude.

Why the Borrowings Matter 11

It is further held that a focus on plagiarism does harm to the status of African literature in general. All of these are reasons why some prefer to ignore the borrowings in *Le Devoir de violence*. But I will argue here that the borrowings (plagiarisms, quotations, cuttings, grafts, *prélèvements*, *démarquages*[8]—call them what you will) are too plentiful *and too meaningful* to be ignored; that they are inseparable from Ouologuem's vision of history; that his novel is a unique construction—a hapax—in which the pillaging of (almost entirely) European literature produces a new vision of Africa.

There is a delicious irony in a phrase used in the snide review of the French original version of *Le Devoir de violence* in the *TLS*. The reviewer (anonymous, following *TLS* custom at the time) wrote: "Nothing written in a European language could be *farther from a European tradition* than *Le Devoir de violence*" (the reviewer deplores the "various treatments of the genitalia ...," the "unsqueamishness," "the wallowing in cruelty and violence itself").[9] In fact, unbeknownst to the reviewer, the novel was saturated with "a European tradition," in the form of thousands of literary words from that tradition, borrowed.

It is also argued that the borrowings "take us back to Europe," and this is indeed literally true, because all but a few of the known source texts are Western in some sense; the only non-Western texts are two Arabic chronicles the *Tarîkh el-Fettach* and the *Tarîkh es-Soudan*, the *Thousand and One Nights*, the Turkish tales of Nasreddin Hodja, and (perhaps) Camara Laye's *Le Regard du roi* (or does that count as Belgian?).[10] It was in Europe that Ouologuem did almost all of his voracious textual hunting and gathering; he used what he used, and it amounts to an astonishingly eclectic array of literature, high and low and middle-brow, from the Bible to modern pornography. But, more importantly, as I will argue, he *transformed* his findings, "Africanizing" them in each case,[11] inventing an Africa that had not been seen before, while turning European literature (and one publishing house) against itself.

History and (inter)textuality are inseparable in *Le Devoir de violence* because of the way Ouologuem worked: in the borrowings themselves, Ouologuem invites us into comparisons and down paths of history that otherwise—if he had written his story "straight"—might not come into view. This makes it incumbent on the reader, I will argue, to open these doors, cross the thresholds, and venture down these paths. The borrowings are a language in which Ouologuem wrote; many of the most powerful and compelling passages in the novel are both *borrowed and adapted*. They are, to use current jargon, "repurposed." *Le Devoir*

12   *Thresholds*

de violence cannot be understood without attention to the art of borrowing, which is inextricably linked to his idea of history—not to mention his astonishingly original concept of the novel. To ignore the borrowings would be like analyzing a painting without discussing the paint or the brushstrokes.[12] No single explanation of this novel can fully account for its complex origins, fabric, and meaning; we can only make attempts to understand it.

This second part of *Thresholds* has several purposes. It serves as an introduction to the table of borrowings that follows in Part Three. The table is intended to be "complete" in a narrow, particular sense: every known borrowing (as of this writing) is included; but the full text of the borrowing is not necessarily included, for reasons of space. This is therefore a *summary* table of the "complete" borrowings. The task of establishing a complete table of borrowings proved more difficult than I had anticipated when I began the project, and when all is said and done, it may remain a quixotic and asymptotic goal. After some flailing about, I came upon the website of Joël Bertrand, a French scholar with an interest in Ouologuem that goes back to the 1980s.[13] Bertrand's wizardry has revealed that the borrowings—his preferred term is *prélèvements*[14]—are far more extensive than scholars had realized; their sheer volume reopens the question of their status and function within the novel, and of this novel as a work of art. Any thought that "the so-called plagiarism occurred in an insignificant portion of the work as a whole" is now obsolete.[15] And Souleymane Bachir Diagne's claim that the "beauty" of the novel "owes very little to the passages spotted as 'plagiarisms'" may need to be reappraised.[16] There is, it must now be admitted, beauty *in* the borrowings.

Many scholars have discovered and exposed borrowings, beginning in 1971; the process appears to be endless.[17] My work here mostly ignores debates about the ethics of borrowing, the legalities of plagiarism, and the nuances among terms like borrowing, intertextuality, and *prélèvement*. Rather, I think it is time for a re-examination of Ouologuem's borrowings *as conduits of meaning*.[18]

My aim is therefore to invite new considerations of the borrowings, not limited to my few suggestions here. I will provide only three examples of the ways in which the borrowings work, in an effort to show why they matter: by Africanization, by polyvocalizing history, and through the question of translation. These are but three among dozens of paths that might be taken through the forest of borrowings that Ouologuem created. But before proceeding, there are several preliminary steps

Why the Borrowings Matter **13**

that must be taken: a few words about the concept of "borrowing"; an overview of the borrowings as they are now known; and a comparison of Ouologuem to the contemporary author from whom he borrowed the most, André Schwarz-Bart.

Can Words Be "Borrowed"?

> After your words—unlike your VCR—are stolen, you still own them.
> Or do you?
>
> Anne Fadiman, "Nothing New Under the Sun," in *Ex Libris: Confessions of a Common Reader*

What does it mean to "borrow" words? It is not the same as borrowing a car or a shovel or a VCR: the words that are borrowed, unlike the car or the shovel, remain in their original place. (Except for neologisms, all words are borrowed; that's how they make sense.) When Yambo Ouologuem borrowed words from André Schwarz-Bart, did those words disappear from all copies of *Le Dernier des Justes*? I don't think so. The original work remained unaltered.[19] Words are not like cars or shovels: when borrowed, they stay right where they were in the first place; they can be in more than one place at the same time. So the observation made by the learned and prolific American judge Richard A. Posner, in his *Little Book of Plagiarism*—"'borrowing,' the term preferred by apologists for plagiarism (and there are such apologists) is misleading, too, since the 'borrowed' material is never returned"[20]—is nonsense. The material is never returned because it was not *removed* in the first place: it was *reproduced*. Textual borrowing arguably (very arguably, since much rides on this point) does nothing to the original text, which remains unaltered. I concede that "borrowing" can be a euphemism for a form of theft and deception. Wholesale appropriation of someone else's work is rightly illegal. But I will argue that what Yambo Ouologuem did was something very different: it *was* borrowing, in an artistic *tour de force* that could not possibly have done harm to any text from which he borrowed. So: *cui malo*? This does not mean that he operated within the laws of copyright; he probably did not. Seuil settled with Harcourt for the puzzling sum of $4,786.12, out of court, on their own, but the question of Ouologuem's legal "guilt" was never, in fact, adjudicated.

Another model for interpreting Ouologuem's practice is that of *constraint*. While plagiarism is typically thought of as an act of laziness,

14   *Thresholds*

a work-saving process of copying and pasting, Ouologuem's method is more like a complication he imposed on himself. We will see instances in which it would have been much easier for him to tell the story "straight," but he didn't.[21] Instead he, first, detoured through a vast array of source materials and borrowed from them. This took work; the borrowings did not just fall from the sky. Ouologuem thereby imposed on himself a second, necessary, "extra" step, that of *adapting* the source text to the context of his novel. This was the opposite of time- or effort-saving. It was not quite like writing a novel that does not contain the letter "e" (as Georges Perec of the OULIPO group did), but it was a constraint.[22]

The role of Ouologuem's adaptive gestures has been underappreciated; they no doubt comprise thousands of words in the novel. My table of borrowings shows dozens of examples: words not in bold are not copied from the source text but are instead paraphrastically related. They are hinges between the source text and the diegesis of *Le Devoir de violence*. Further, these acts of adaptation set Ouologuem's practice apart from pure collage, which does not blend materials together but rather leaves them intact and discrete.[23]

To be clear; a word to students and writers of all kinds: do not plagiarize! If you borrow the ideas or words of others, you must acknowledge it. What Yambo Ouologuem did was an act of civil disobedience, a purposeful flouting of the rules, an attack on the Parisian literary establishment. He could have set things right by acknowledging his sources, even belatedly, but he chose not to, thus standing fast with the "open" secrecy of his artistic practice, likely to the detriment of his own best interests. For this, he suffered the consequences.

And, to put this question of borrowing into a larger context, it should be stipulated that, for African writers, French is (still) a "borrowed" language. French remains a language of power, and French literary institutions continue to control the means of production and reward. They give, they take away. This fact stands in tension with another: that "French has become an African language."[24] But in literature particularly, Paris continues to reign. Francophone authors, and authors who are fully French but of even partial African descent, are constantly reminded of this centralized power. The case of Marie NDiaye and the controversy that surrounded her Prix Goncourt in 2009—by sheer dint of her perceived identity—and its implications for her right to criticize the government, comes to mind.[25]

Why the Borrowings Matter   15

Francophone Literary Borrowing and "Textual Ownership"

Borrowing should be seen within a larger spectrum of creative intertextual practices: influence, allusion, wink, echo, imitation, parody, pastiche, and so on. These tropes are everywhere in literature. Borrowing goes one step further, away from sanctioned literary practice and toward risk; plagiarism is an actual violation of the law.

To describe Ouologuem's writing practice as unique is not to say that it was without analogous precedents and successors. Francophone African literature has been haunted by questions of "textual ownership"—most notably ghostwriting and plagiarism—since its beginnings.[26] One of the first novels, *Force-Bonté*, was probably not written by its listed author, Bakary Diallo; and serious questions have been raised about two of the most famous works in the canon, Camara Laye's *L'Enfant noir* and *Le Regard du roi*.[27]

Dominic Thomas writes: "Francophone writers have invariably found themselves ensnared in complex creative circumstances requiring a mediation with established aesthetic connections ... In turn, many [of these] writers have challenged and even played with these assumptions in their attempt to confuse these power relations."[28] Textual borrowing, in some cases, is a means used by Francophone authors to challenge the status quo. It can also be plain old plagiarism, artless and corrupt.

The case of Yambo Ouologuem is that of a writer who found the circumstances of publishing intolerable and formulated a particularly radical, decolonial "challenge" to them. I will argue that his response was unique, and remains unequaled; yet it should be seen within this larger context in which authors purposefully rebel against literary conventions and strictures, particularly as they pertain to issues of ownership. I will briefly summarize a few cases, one from before *Le Devoir de violence*, the others from after.

Ousmane Sembene's novel *Le Docker noir*, published in 1956, tells a remarkable story of an African immigrant living in Marseille who writes a book only to have it "stolen" by a white French woman, whom he then kills. The question of textual ownership is thus at the heart of the tale, and, as Dominic Thomas suggests, it is then compounded by the fact, later discovered, that Sembene borrowed passages from Richard Wright's *Native Son* (significantly, from its French translation). Plagiarism is, Thomas argues, "at the very center of the text's concerns."[29]

There is a huge difference between Sembene's borrowing in *Le Docker noir* and Ouologuem's in *Le Devoir de violence*, starting with

16 Thresholds

scale: the borrowing in the earlier novel was limited to a few passages, from only one source. Sembene's borrowing (beyond mere "influence") from Wright was not discovered until long after the fact, and it caused no scandal, provoking only calm discussion among scholars. Sembene endured no consequences.[30]

This, in turn, stands in contrast to a more recent case. About 25 years after the Ouologuem affair, another African Francophone writer was accused of plagiarism: Calixthe Beyala, a prominent novelist born in Cameroon and living in Paris. In 1992 Beyala was accused of plagiarism by an American novelist, Howard Buten. In 1996, she was convicted in a French court for having plagiarized some 40 passages from Buten's *When I Was Five I Killed Myself*, or rather from its French translation, *Quand j'avais cinq ans, je m'ai tué* [sic]. In a rare occurrence, she was fined a total of 100,000 francs.

Then, an exposé in the magazine *Lire* in 1997 revealed extensive further borrowings by Beyala from Romain Gary (*La Vie devant soi*), Paule Constant (*White Spirit*), Alice Walker (*The Color Purple*, French translation), and Ben Okri (*Famished Road*, French translation).[31] Beyala said the accusations were "racist." This *was* a scandal and an "affaire," with real legal consequences for the author. Nikki Hitchcott compares the cases of Ouologuem and Beyala:

> What is perhaps most striking about the difference between them are the reactions by the two authors and the subsequent effects on their publishing careers. Whereas, despite protests of innocence, Ouologuem's novel was withdrawn from sale for thirty years and the author retreated into literary silence, Calixthe Beyala continued to make the bestseller lists for her five subsequent novels, and has become something of a minor celebrity on French TV and radio.[32]

The contrast is thus mirror-like: Ouologuem's case was never adjudicated but resulted in the end of his career; Beyala was found guilty of plagiarism and fined, but she carried on, uninterrupted in her glamorous trajectory until 2014, when she published her last novel.[33] It would be difficult to make the argument that Beyala was anything but a plagiarist; to my knowledge no one has tried.

The intertextual practices of Congolese writers Henri Lopes and Sony Labou Tansi are complex and intriguing; they have been explored in depth by others. Lopes borrowed from the autobiography—*My Country, Africa*—by the Central African activist and author Andrée Blouin, in his novel *Le Lys et le flamboyant*.[34] Sony Labou Tansi seems to have borrowed from novellas by Lopes in order to construct some of the plays for his Rocado Zulu Theater; and he himself suggested that his novel *La Vie et demie* was a rewriting of Lopes's *Le Pleurer-Rire*.[35] Exchanging signifiers promiscuously, a "Congolese brotherhood" of authors thrived in the late twentieth century. Later, this rich national tradition would be joined by Alain Mabanckou, whose novel *Verre cassé* is a veritable compendium of literary allusions.[36]

But these are all epiphenomena. None of these writers used the art of borrowing exactly the way Yambo Ouologuem did, to such an extent, to such effect, nor with such lasting consequences. There is no other Ouologuem.

An Overview of the Borrowings

An analytical look at Joël Bertrand's work reveals the following salient points:

- There are 37 known instances of borrowing in *Le Devoir de violence*: see Figure 1. Some of these instances are enormously complex, involving fragmented verbatim passages interrupted by Ouologuem's original prose. Other readers might choose to count the instances of borrowing in different ways.

- There appear to be 29 discrete author-sources (an author-source being either an individual or a collective text such as the two African Arabic chronicles): see Figure 2. They comprise many different models of authorship, from ancient to modern, individual and collective, copyrighted and public domain.

- These numbers (37 and 29) are not of great value, since they are likely to change as more sources are identified, and also for the following reason.

- The borrowings are of radically varying dimensions: on the one hand, only two words are taken from the novel attributed to Camara Laye, *Le Regard du roi* (published in English as *The Radiance of the King*); on the other hand, Ouologuem borrowed thousands of words from Maupassant. And of course the entire novel is built on references to and extensive borrowings from André Schwarz-Bart's *Le Dernier des Justes*.

18 *Thresholds*

- In some cases the borrowing seems trivial, as if for form only, or as some kind of private joke: the cases of Violette Leduc and "A. Waltraut" are among these needles in haystacks found by Bertrand.

- "The Ecstasy and the Agony" can barely be considered a borrowing; it is a simple allusion to the novel by Irving Stone.

- In other cases, Ouologuem borrowed a major plot point, essential in the source text and in *Le Devoir de violence* as well. When the protagonist Raymond Kassoumi realizes that he has slept with his own sister, a prostitute, the words and situation are borrowed from Maupassant's "Le Port" (see the table).

- Only one author, Violette Leduc, is a woman.

- The number and the sheer magnitude of the borrowings should lay to rest any notion that the novel can be read without taking them into account, or that they are some kind of parlor trick without significance. Across more than 50 years, Ouologuem is telling us to pay attention to this aspect of his work.

A quick glance at, or perhaps a longer perusal of, the table of borrowings suggests multiple paths of exploration and interpretation. How many possibilities open up before one's eyes?[37] Why did Ouologuem make these choices? What do these texts have in common, if anything? (For example, two of the Anglophone novels share a plot device: both Greene's *It's a Battlefield* and MacDonald's *The Edge of Night* are framed by an impending execution. Was Ouologuem intrigued by that?)

What processes of transformation and adaptation did Ouologuem use, beyond simple cut-and-paste? My three themes are offered as a partial gloss on the would-be complete table of borrowings that follows: Africanization, polyvocality, and translation. Each of these, I want to argue, is a threshold, a portal of meaning. A borrowing is a portal, leading to a different universe. (It shares this effect with hoaxes.)[38] Ouologuem's borrowings transport us from the African empire of "Nakem" to York, England in the Middle Ages; from Africa to Uvalde, Texas; to Bavaria; and to Hong Kong; from Paris in the twentieth century to Marseille in the nineteenth; and so on.

See Joel Bertrand, http://joelbertrand.wordpress.com/436-2/

1. Baldwin, James. *Another Country/Un Autre pays.*
2. *Book of Chronicles.*
3. Camara Laye (attributed to, unresolved). *Le Regard du roi.*
4. Césaire, Aimé. *Cahier d'un retour au pays natal.*
5. Chandler, Raymond. *The Big Sleep/Le Grand sommeil.*
6. Delafosse, Maurice. *Haut-Sénégal-Niger.*
7. Flaubert, Gustave. "La Légende de Saint-Julien l'Hospitalier."
8. Frobenius, Leo. *Histoire de la civilization africaine,* French translation.
9. *Genesis.*
10. Greene, Graham. *It's a Battlefield/C'est un champ de bataille.*
11. John. *The Gospel According to John.*
12. Leduc, Violette. *Thérèse et Isabelle.*
13. Leiris, Michel. *L'Afrique fantôme.*
14. MacDonald, John D. *The Edge of the Night/Les Energumènes.*
15. Mark. *The Gospel According to Mark.*
16. Matthew. *The Gospel According to Matthew.*
17. *One Thousand and One Nights.*
18. Nasreddin Hodja, tales of.

Maupassant, Guy de. Nine stories, by order of appearance in *Le Devoir de violence*

19. "Boule de suif."
20. "Le Champ d'oliviers."
21. "L'Aveugle."
22. "Le Gueux."
23. "Le Port."
24. "Marroca."
25. "Le Rosier de Mme Husson."
26. "Monsieur Parent."
27. "La Chevelure."
28. Paul (Saint). *Letter to the Galatians.*
29. Robbe-Grillet, Alain. *La Maison de rendez-vous.*
30. Schwarz-Bart, André. *Le Dernier des justes.*
31. Stone, Irving. *The Agony and the Ecstasy.*
32. *Tarîkh el-Fettach.*
33. *Tarîkh es-Soudan.*
34. Suret-Canale, Jean. *Afrique Noire Occidentale et Centrale: géographie, civilizations, histoire.* (Quoting from Vigné d'Octon, below.)
35. Roussier, Paul. *L'Etablissement d'Issiny 1687-1702.*
36. Vigné d'Octon. *La Gloire du sabre.* (Quoted in Suret-Canale.)
37. A. Waltraut, *La Bavaroise.*

Figure 1. "All" text sources in *Le Devoir de violence*.

20 Thresholds

A. THE 29 DISCRETE SOURCE-AUTHORS IN *LE DEVOIR DE VIOLENCE*

See Joel Bertrand, http://joelbertrand.wordpress.com/436-2/

1. Baldwin, James. *Another Country/Un Autre pays.*
2. *Book of Chronicles.*
3. Camara Laye (attributed to, unresolved). *Le Regard du roi.*
4. Césaire, Aimé. *Cahier d'un retour au pays natal.*
5. Chandler, Raymond. *The Big Sleep/Le Grand sommeil.*
6. Delafosse, Maurice. *Haut-Sénégal-Niger.*
7. Flaubert, Gustave. "La Légende de Saint-Julien l'Hospitalier."
8. Frobenius, Leo. *Histoire de la civilization africaine,* French translation.
9. *Genesis.*
10. Greene, Graham. *It's a Battlefield/ C'est un champ de bataille.*
11. John. *The Gospel According to John.*
12. Leduc, Violette. *Thérèse et Isabelle.*
13. Leiris, Michel. *L'Afrique fantôme.*
14. MacDonald, John D. *The Edge of the Night/Les Energumènes.*
15. Mark. *The Gospel According to Mark.*
16. Matthew. *The Gospel According to Matthew.*
17. *One Thousand and One Nights.*
18. Nasreddin Hodja, tales of.
19. Maupassant, Guy de. Nine different works; see Figure 1.
20. Paul (Saint). *Letter to the Galatians.*
21. Robbe-Grillet, Alain. *La Maison de rendez-vous.*
22. Schwarz-Bart, André. *Le Dernier des justes.*
23. Stone, Irving. *The Agony and the Ecstasy.*
24. *Tarîkh el-Fettach.*
25. *Tarîkh es-Soudan.*
26. Suret-Canale, Jean. *Afrique Noire Occidentale et Centrale: géographie, civilizations, histoire.*
27. Roussier, Paul. *L'Etablissement d'Issiny 1687-1702.*
28. Vigné d'Octon, Paul. *La Gloire du sabre.* (Quoted in Suret-Canale.)
29. "A. Waltraut," *La Bavaroise.*

Figure 2a.

> B. DEMOGRAPHIC ANALYSIS OF SOURCE-AUTHORS
> - 11 French (including Césaire, and counting Suret-Canale and Vigné d'Octon as two, and including the unknown "A. Waltraut")
> - 3 African (Camara Laye and the two chronicles)
> - 2 Francophone authors (Camara and Césaire)
> - 4 American (including one African American: Baldwin)
> - 1 British (Greene)
> - 1 German (Frobenius)
> - 1 African-Caribbean/Antillean: Césaire
> - 5 Anglophone (the Americans and Greene)
> - 1 woman (Leduc)
> - 6 Biblical
> - 2 traditional tales

Figure 2b.

The Schwarz-Bart Connection, and a Comparison

Borrowings from André Schwarz-Bart's 1959 novel *Le Dernier des Justes* begin and end *Le Devoir de violence*, lending this a special status in the table of intertexts, as a kind of shadow frame tale. The amount of borrowing from Schwarz-Bart is very extensive and may not yet be fully documented.[39] I actually want to comment first not on the textual connections, but on an important comparison between the two authors and their actions after the publication of their respective novels. I do not think this comparison has been adequately delineated.[40]

The parallels between these two writers are almost uncanny. In both cases, after a novel was published, there were accusations of both ideological aberrancy and plagiarism. Everything unfolded as if some of the literary DNA of Schwarz-Bart's book had passed into Ouologuem's novel along with the borrowed words: first, a *succès d'estime*, followed by an important literary prize; then *succès de scandale*, questions of plagiarism and inauthenticity; and ultimately in both cases, exile from the Parisian literary scene and the suppression (if not destruction) of a literary career. There are nuances within each case and differences between them, but that much remains true.

Le Dernier des Justes turned into the "Affaire Schwarz-Bart" in 1959, and for a time in the fall of that year, his Goncourt was hanging

22 Thresholds

by a thread. Accused of plagiarism ("borrowings, sometimes word for word, from other authors"),[41] of ignorance, of cultural if not religious apostasy, and of writing "a Christian book" disguised as a Jewish one, Schwarz-Bart then did what Ouologuem later refused to do: he defended himself thoroughly and effectively; in later editions he corrected some errors and included a list of his sources. Still, the "Affaire Schwarz-Bart"—with 300 articles published between the publication of *Le Dernier des Justes* and the announcement of the Prix Goncourt in December, and many more thereafter[42]—took its toll on the author. "Undone by the misunderstandings surrounding his work and its meaning," writes Francine Kaufmann, "he decides to leave France in February 1960 and to destroy all his manuscripts in 1962."[43] After time in Israel, Senegal, and Switzerland, he spent the rest of his life in Guadeloupe with his wife, Simone Schwarz-Bart, with whom he collaborated and who became a writer in her own right.[44] He co-authored one book with Simone, and published another under his sole signature, *La Mulâtresse Solitude*, in 1972. He continued to write, but nothing more was published until after his death.[45]

Less than ten years later, Yambo Ouologuem, having borrowed heavily from Schwarz-Bart's *Le Dernier des Justes*, followed the same literary path, with the same publisher and similar scandals. He, too, ended his literary career, under circumstances that were far harsher than those suffered by Schwarz-Bart. Both writers were in a sense chewed up and spat out by the Parisian literary machine.[46] Meanwhile, Schwarz-Bart's generosity with regard to Ouologuem (he said, "I have always seen my books as apple trees, and I am happy that others eat my apples ... and plant them in other soil")[47] may have stemmed from his own experience of having been accused of plagiarism in 1959.

Counterfactually, what if Schwarz-Bart had exercised his authorial rights and sued both Seuil and Ouologuem? It is entirely possible that *Le Devoir de violence* would never have been printed in the first place.

I now turn to my three case studies, illustrations of ways in which Ouologuem's borrowings work as thresholds of discovery and meaning.

Why the Borrowings Matter **23**

Case Studies

1. Africanization

Africanization was one of Ouologuem's most frequent adaptive gestures. This was necessary with most of his borrowings for the simple reason that the source text was European, set in a European context with European characters (or American). In order to set *Le Devoir de violence* mostly in Africa, with African characters (even the scenes that take place in France), it was necessary for people and things to "become" African—or at least compatible with the physical and cultural environment of the Africa that Ouologuem wanted to create.

This process did not take place in an editorial vacuum. Early readers of Ouologuem's manuscripts at Editions du Seuil were disappointed to find nothing "African" in his writing. The young man had been bombarding Seuil with manuscripts, including an early novel also called *Le Devoir de violence* that had nothing to do with Africa; between 1963 and 1967 he sent them "at least" three manuscripts as well as a volume of poetry.[48] Nothing was accepted. Ouologuem ran headlong into the systemic racism of French publishing. Some of the readers' reports were scathing and racist: "It is a parrot, not a man, who tried to write this novel *à la française*."[49] A parrot is a bird that talks, in imitation of human speech. The trope of imitativeness, of copying, is highly fraught in a colonial context, and far from innocent. The colonized, particularly an individual who rose high in the educational system, was mocked as a "bad copy" of the colonizer.[50] It is no coincidence that Ouologuem's method of textual collage and borrowing—invented, no doubt, in reaction to these readings—threw this racist metaphor back in the colonizer's face, *by copying*. He did the very thing of which he was accused, but surreptitiously and defiantly.

As Sarah Burnautzki has argued, this was a case of "racial profiling" in the halls of Parisian publishing. In order to get published, Ouologuem was forced to "Africanize" his writing, if not himself. He did this, but literally with a vengeance: I will be African if you insist, but my novel will be built out of the shards of your own literature.[51] That at least is one interpretation of his practice. While to some this explanation may smack of *post hoc ergo propter hoc*, the textual evidence—which shows Africanization on almost every page—supports it, and it was part of a process that ran through several of his manuscripts in succession until reaching its apogee in *Le Devoir de violence*. When the final version

24 Thresholds

came along, one reader for Seuil hailed it, with reservations, as an "African *In Search of Lost Time*."[52]

While still refusing to publish *Le Devoir*, the editor François-Régis Bastide had some advice for Ouologuem: instead of relying on "archaic French turns of phrase," you must "find African equivalents."[53] Let us pause for a moment to consider Bastide's well-meaning gesture; it needs to be placed in the history of what Noémie Ndiaye calls "scripts of blackness." Ndiaye recounts what her acting teacher, "trying to help," told her in 2008: "It's not working because you are not being African enough for the part."[54] Bastide's advice to Ouologuem 40 years earlier was part of this tradition with deep roots (going back, as Ndiaye demonstrates, to the early modern period) and great longevity: the requirement for Africans to satisfy Western standards of Africanness. Between the accusation of being a parrot and not a man, on the one hand, and of being "not African enough" on the other, Ouologuem was clearly caught in a web of Western tropes, a "script of blackness," with no clear path forward.

In response, Ouologuem didn't simply flip the script; he wrote an entirely new one. He invented a path of his own. He found "African equivalents," that is certain, although not of the kind that Bastide had in mind. Rather, the novelist chose to *Africanize European texts*, taking the accusation of imitativeness ("parroting") into a hall of mirrors that he alone controlled, and where he invisibly ran circles around his editors and readers. In the process, he altered the genre of the novel, in ways that we continue to discover. The contract was signed on October 11, 1967, and the book appeared the following year.

The exact implications and contours of what Ouologuem did through his manipulation of borrowed texts are difficult to define. He was subversive, an insurgent, a rebel, a Prometheus: all those things. While "Africanizing," he was not content—unlike Senghor and Césaire— to deploy an "invented," ready-made Africa received from European sources like Leo Frobenius; his Africa would be radically different.[55] In more contemporary terms taken from Walter D. Mignolo and Catherine E. Walsh, he was a *decolonial disrupter* in French publishing.[56] But none of these notions capture the *surreptitious* nature of his work, which complicated the results both for him and for us, all these years later. Hence this study, and no doubt other studies to come.

So there is a huge difference between the kind of "Africanization" that Seuil asked for and the kind that Ouologuem delivered. And that was his tricksterish genius, to pull off this substitution right in Seuil's own house, under their noses. *I won't just Africanize by writing about Africa, "like an African," whatever that means to you; I will Africanize your literature, starting with one of Seuil's own prize works, your first Goncourt, Le Dernier des justes.* By doing this, by borrowing, Ouologuem became an integral part of one of the most important trends in mid-century art: that of appropriation (now under threat from the United States Supreme Court).[57] Copying, collage, embedding someone else's photograph, sampling in music: all of these are characteristic of the late twentieth century, and Ouologuem was an integral, if underappreciated, part of this global trend. An art historian wrote of Warhol words that could apply to Ouologuem: "Throughout his career, the artist was concerned not with copyright but with *the right to copy*, which he saw both as a creative method and a design for living."[58]

(The counterexample here, in terms of African writing in French—and Africans writing *à l'africaine*—is Ahmadou Kourouma, who wrote in a new "African" style (Malinke, actually), of his own invention and volition, at the same time. Ironically, his brilliant first novel, *Les Soleils des indépendances*, was refused by Seuil and numerous other houses, finally published in Montreal in 1968, then picked up by none other than Seuil two years later.)[59]

As *Le Devoir de violence* opens, the text immediately becomes a parody of André Schwarz-Bart's novel, published by Seuil only a few years earlier. The source text opens in medieval England (words that are reproduced from *Le Dernier des Justes* in *Le Devoir de violence* are in bold):

> **Nos yeux** reçoivent la lumière d'étoiles mortes. Une biographie de mon ami Ernie **tiendrait aisément** dans le deuxième quart du XXe siècle; mais **la véritable histoire** d'Ernie Lévy **commence** très **tôt**, vers **l'an mille de notre ère, dans** la cité anglicane de York. Plus précisément: le 11 mars 1185.[60]

> Our eyes register the light of dead stars. A biography of my friend Ernie could easily be set in the second quarter of the twentieth century, but the true history of Ernie Levy begins much earlier, toward the year 1000 of our era, in the old Anglican city of York. More precisely, on March 11, 1185.[61]

In Ouologuem's adaptation, England becomes "African":

> **Nos yeux** boivent l'éclat du soleil, et, vaincus, s'étonnent de pleurer. *Maschallah! oua bismillah!* ... Un récit de l'aventure sanglante de la négraille—honte aux hommes de rien!—**tiendrait aisément dans**

26   Thresholds

la première moitié de ce siècle; mais **la véritable histoire** des Nègres **commence** beaucoup, beaucoup plus **tôt,** avec les Saïfs, **en l'an 1202 de notre ère, dans** l'Empire africain de Nakem, au Sud du Fezzan, bien après les conquêtes d'Okba ben Nafi el Fitri.[62]

Our eyes drink the brightness of the sun, and, overcome, marvel at their tears. *Mashallah! wa bismillah!* ... To recount the bloody adventure of the niggertrash [*sic*]—shame to the worthless paupers!—there would be no need to go back beyond the present century; but the true history of the Blacks begins much earlier, with the Saifs, in the year 1202 of our era, in the African Empire of Nakem south of Fezzan, long after the conquests of Okba ben Nafi al-Fitri.[63]

The point for now is a simple one: in order to rewrite (and copy) *Le Dernier des Justes* for Africa, Ouologuem took an "Anglican" city and made it an African empire. There are hundreds of examples of this trope in *Le Devoir*: "l'intérêt général" in *Le Dernier des Justes* (14) becomes "le romantisme nègre" in *Le Devoir* (14); a street light in Greene's *It's a Battlefield* (French translation, 87) becomes a pressurized (kerosene) lamp in *Le Devoir* (95); a car seat in John D. MacDonald's *The End of the Night* (130; trans. 166) becomes a rock in *Le Devoir* (130); "roots" in Flaubert's *La Légende de Saint Julien l'Hospitalier* become yams ("ignames") in *Le Devoir* (141). In other instances, Ouologuem adds something specific from African history, thereby Africanizing, for example, a passage from Maupassant's "Le Gueux": he adds that a woman's parents had "died under forced labor in the colonizers' work camps" (155, trans. 135).[64] And of course there is the changing of many Western names to African ones. In some cases, I am convinced that Ouologuem was laughing out loud as he, for example, turned a jet plane (from MacDonald's *The End of the Night*) into a hyena, or, in the same scene, a can of shaving cream into a viper (see table). There are your "African equivalents"!

But this begs the larger question of interpretation. What does it mean to take the history of European Jews and transpose it to Africa, even while making the highly ambiguous gesture—perhaps another joke on Ouologuem's part—of making the ruling dynasty of the Nakem empire, the Saïfs, Jewish? This brings us back to Schwarz-Bart's *Le Dernier des Justes*. In fact, the Saïfs merely *claim* to be Jewish;[65] the gesture may be yet another dig at anthropology, and specifically Maurice Delafosse's claim that the Peul people are Jewish in origin.[66] This in turn begs another question: that of the negative depiction of the

Why the Borrowings Matter   27

hideous Saïf dynasty as even putatively or self-styled Jewish. If a faint odor of anti-Semitism hangs in the air, it is hardly the only example of Ouologuem playing with ideological fire.

Each act of borrowing is a portal, an invitation to reflection, a comparison that Ouologuem wants us to consider. A thorough analysis of the analogy between Jewish history and African history—fundamental to the structure of *Le Devoir de violence*—has yet to be done.[67] That portal of meaning invites future work. But it is also important to note that Ouologuem's technique—as if playing on the name of his publishing house—leaves us on the *threshold* of discovery. He does not take us through the door; that is for us to do on our own.

2. Textual Borrowing and Polyvocal History

By examining one particularly rich example, I hope to demonstrate Ouologuem's interweaving of textuality and history and how it produces polyvocality. This is a case in which one borrowing is the threshold for an important portal of meaning, a door to history. I want to go through a door that Ouologuem left ajar, and to explore what is behind it, namely an event of enormous importance in the history of West Africa. No critic of *Le Devoir de violence* has discussed this.

Behind the question of polyvocality in *Le Devoir* stands the tradition of the West African griots, whose individual voices over the centuries have borrowed from each other in richly interweaving and repetitive patterns. Ouologuem's acts of textual borrowing need to be seen in this historical and cultural context. The narrator of the novel often speaks like a griot ("Or, voyez ...," "Voyez encore ...," 12). Thomas Hale's analysis shows how Ouologuem borrowed and altered the content of West African oral traditions and the two written chronicles, the *Tarîkh el-Fettach* and the *Tarîkh es-Soudan*. As an example of Ouologuem's complex polyvocal practice, Hale shows how the author "compressed time considerably, reducing many generations and hundreds of pages of the chronicles into his twenty-three-page first chapter."[68] Much more detail can be found in Hale's chapter, especially his section on "The Multiple Voices of Ouologuem's Narrator."

In one of the most horrific passages of the novel, Ouologuem describes the aftermath of a French military conquest in West Africa, with reference to 1898. The French are called "the foreigners" or "the Whites"; *tirailleurs* are African soldiers recruited by the French; "Africa is there, watchful [*aux aguets*]," the narrator says. Without specifying

28   *Thresholds*

an exact location for what follows, Ouologuem writes and borrows (borrowed words are in bold):

> **Tout est pris,** saccagé, volé—et **les captifs,** au nombre de huit mille environ, sont **rassemblés en un troupeau** dont le **colonel commence la distribution. Il écrivait lui-même sur un calepin, puis y renonçait,** clamant: "**Partagez-vous cela!**"
>
> Et **chaque Blanc obtint plus de dix femmes noires à son choix. Retour** au quartier général en **étapes de quarante kilomètres avec** les **captifs. Enfants, malades ou invalides: tués à coups de crosse et de baïonnette. Et leurs cadavres, laissés au bord de la route. Une femme est trouvée accroupie. Elle est enceinte. On la pousse,** on la bouscule à coups de genoux. Elle accouche debout en marchant. **A** peine **coupé le cordon** et jeté, d'un coup de pied, hors de la route, l'enfant, l'on avance, sans s'inquiéter de la mère hagarde qui boitille, délire, titube, vagissant, puis tombant, cent mètres plus loin, écrasée par la foule.

> [...]

> Les Nègres réquisitionnés en route pour porter le mil restent cinq jours sans rations; reçoivent quarante coups de cravache s'ils prélèvent une poignée des dix à vingt-cinq kilos de vivres qu'ils portent sur leurs têtes nues, rasées. **Les tirailleurs, le commun des soldats, les sous-officiers et officiers ont tant d'esclaves qu'il leur est impossible de les compter, les loger ou les nourrir.** (37)

Ralph Manheim's English translation reads:

> They pillage, loot, destroy everything in their path—the captives, some eight thousand of them, are herded together and the colonel, writing in his little black book, starts to apportion them. But then he gives up and shouts: "Go on, divide 'em up."
>
> And each white man chooses for himself more than ten black women. Return to base with captives in daily marches of twenty-five miles. The children, the sick and disabled are killed with rifle butts and bayonets, their corpses abandoned by the roadside. A woman is found squatting. Big with child. They push her, prod her with their knees. She gives birth standing up, marching. The umbilical cord is cut, the child kicked off the road, and the column marches on, heedless of the delirious whimpering mother, who, limping and staggering, finally falls a hundred yards farther on and is crushed by the crowd. (27)

Christine Chaulet-Achour sourced this borrowing to a book by the French Marxist Africanist historian Jean Suret-Canale, *Afrique Noire Occidentale et Centrale: géographie, civilisation, histoire*:

Tout est pris ou tué. Tous les captifs, 4000 environ, rassemblés en troupeau. Le colonel commence la distribution. Il écrivait lui-même sur un calepin, puis il y renonce en disant: "Partagez-vous cela". Le partage a lieu avec dispute et coups. Puis, en route! Chaque Européen a reçu une femme à son choix … On a fait au retour des étapes de quarante kilomètres avec ces captifs. Les enfants et tous ceux qui sont fatigués sont tués à coups de crosse et de baïonnette …

Les cadavres étaient laissés au bord des routes. Une femme est trouvée accroupie. Elle est enceinte. On la pousse à coups de crosse. Elle accouche debout en marchant. A coupé le cordon et abandonné [*sic*] l'enfant sans se retourner pour voir si c'était garçon ou fille.

Dans ces mêmes étapes, les hommes **réquisitionnés en route pour porter le mil restent cinq jours sans rations; reçoivent** cinquante **coups de** corde s'ils prennent une poignée de mil qu'ils portent.

Les tirailleurs ont eu tellement de captifs qu'il leur était impossible de les loger et de les nourrir.[69]

But in fact, the words reproduced here are not Suret-Canale's. A footnote, overlooked by Chaulet-Achour, takes us to a work by Paul Vigné d'Octon, a medical doctor, deputy in the National Assembly, and ubiquitous colonial and "anticolonial" writer (author of works like *Au Pays des fétiches* and *Terre de mort: Soudan et Dahomey*)—a gadfly who also published numerous novels, one of which won the prize of the Académie Française.[70] The book quoted here is *La Gloire du sabre* (1900), an outraged indictment of French *military* colonialism. The title is bitterly ironic; his preface is cheekily addressed to the Minister of Colonies. The passage quoted by Suret-Canale describes the French conquest of Sikasso, in what is now Mali; it is worth pausing here to review this event of capital importance in African history: this is what Ouologuem tacitly invited us to do.

Figure 3, showing the page from Suret-Canale that quotes Vigné d'Octon, demonstrates how this works on the textual level. The word "Sikasso" precedes the passage, establishing the context (and is the very first word after the indented quotation, on the next page, as well). That word is not included in the passages that Ouologuem appropriated, so "Sikasso" is missing (as is the name of the king, Ba Bemba) from *Le Devoir de violence*, but only in name. This is what I call Ouologuem's invitation for us to think about Sikasso: he leads us up to the word, the threshold, but requires that we open it up, go inside, and explore. His practice throws the burden, the work, back onto the reader.

Sikasso was the capital of the kingdom of Kénédougou, which was founded in 1825, ethnically Senoufo but ruled by a Dioula dynasty named

30 Thresholds

---

240   *Afrique noire occidentale et centrale*

---

avait aussi les esclaves, achetés aux traitants, et qui vraisemblablement constituèrent, avant que les levées « régulières » fussent possibles, la masse des combattants. Dans les campagnes du Soudan, lorsque se faisait sentir le besoin d'effectifs supplémentaires, on opérait de la manière suivante : au poste, était ouvert le registre des « engagements volontaires »; les marchands d'esclaves prévenus amenaient leur « marchandise »; le captif en bonne condition de service était acheté en général (dans les années 1895-1900) pour moins de 300 francs. Vendu contre reçu et signature d'un « acte de libération », le malheureux captif était censé, après avoir été « libéré », s'être « engagé volontairement ». De gibier, il devenait chasseur.

Un officier français, participant à la prise de Sikasso, décrit ainsi le « sac » de la ville :

> Après le siège, l'assaut. Ba Bemba se tue. On donne l'ordre du pillage. Tout est pris ou tué. Tous les captifs, 4.000 environ, rassemblés en troupeau.
>
> Le colonel[1] commence la distribution. Il écrivait lui-même sur un calepin, puis y a renoncé en disant : « Partagez-vous cela. » Le partage a eu lieu avec disputes et coups. Puis, en route ! Chaque Européen a reçu une femme à son choix... On a fait au retour des étapes de quarante kilomètres avec ces captifs. Les enfants et tous ceux qui sont fatigués sont tués à coups de crosse et de baïonnette...
>
> Les cadavres étaient laissés au bord des routes. Une femme est trouvée accroupie. Elle est enceinte. On la pousse à coup de crosse. Elle accouche debout en marchant. A coupé le cordon et abandonné l'enfant sans se retourner pour voir si c'était garçon ou fille.
>
> Dans ces mêmes étapes, les hommes réquisitionnés en route pour porter le mil restent cinq jours sans rations; reçoivent cinquante coups de corde s'ils prennent une poignée de mil qu'ils portent.
>
> Les tirailleurs ont eu tellement de captifs qu'il leur était impossible de les loger et de les nourrir...[2]

---

1. Audéoud.
2. Cité par P. Vigné d'Octon : *o. c.*, p. 131 et suivantes (« Notes d'un témoin de la prise de Sikasso »).

Figure 3. Jean Suret-Canale, *Afrique Noire Occidentale et Centrale: géographie, civilisation, histoire*, 2nd ed. (Paris: Editions Sociales, 1961), 1:240.

Traoré, with a population that was only partially made up of converts to Islam in the nineteenth century.[71] Sikasso was built into a formidable fortified city, a "veritable citadel" of 90 hectares by 1885, surrounded by a *tata* with crenellated walls 7 or 8 meters tall, a marvel of engineering and architecture.[72] This was done under the reign of the Fama (king) Tiéba Traoré, who was much admired by the French,[73] starting in 1877. Under Tiéba's leadership, Sikasso repelled a 15-month siege by Samory Touré, the conquering and formidable ruler of the Wassoulou Empire and Almamy of the "Dioula Revolution," in 1888, thereby weakening Samory and preparing his empire for its ultimate defeat by the French ten years later.[74] But all along, Tiéba understood that France's war with Samory was a warning to him and to Kénédougou.[75] He died unexpectedly on January 26, 1893. Under the rule of Tiéba's brother and successor, Ba Bemba (see Figure 4)—*not* admired by the French—Sikasso was further expanded, to 240 hectares, and fortified even more. Ba Bemba feinted, telling the French he was their "servant and slave."[76] But there could be no doubt about France's ultimate purpose: the complete conquest of this part of Africa. It was just a matter of time.

How did France, in 1898, come up with a *casus belli* against a kingdom it had supported just a few years earlier? The French sent their final mission to Sikasso in January 1898, led by a Captain Morrison; this was "an attempt to peacefully subjugate Kenedugu by means of political treaties."[77] But Ba Bemba sent the French packing, saying, "I don't want you to stay here to spy on me. I am accountable to no one and fear no one. I will pay no more taxes … I no longer wish to taste the honey of your words. I am king here." A Malian historian describes Ba Bemba as "courageous, but no diplomat."[78] Talks ended with an exchange of threats, and the departing French envoy, Morrison, was marauded in open country outside Sikasso: according to one source, he was stripped naked, circumcised, painted indigo, and given facial scars.[79] An imperial French historian writing in 1901 made it clear that the mistreatment of Morrison was the cause of war.[80]

Morrison then returned to Sikasso as part of the conquering *colonne*. Sikasso fell on May 1, 1898. In half a day, modern French artillery made quick work of the city walls of Sikasso (see Figures 5 and 6).[81] Ba Bemba was said (by some) to have committed suicide rather than face defeat.[82] The French had divided to conquer (see Figure 7). Thus the French vanquished "the last independent city in the Sudan,"[83] and it is the horrific aftermath of that defeat that is described in the passage from Vigné d'Octon, quoted by Suret-Canale, and reproduced by Ouologuem.

Figure 4. "Au milieu, Tiéba, roi du Kénédougou. A gauche, son frère Ba Bemba, qui, plus tard, sera son successeur" (In the middle, Tiéba, king of Kénédougou. On the left, his brother Ba Bemba, who will later succeed him). From Jacques Méniaud, *Les Pionniers du Soudan: avant, avec et après Archinard, 1879–1894* (Paris: Société des Publications Modernes, 1931), 1:371.

Figure 5. "A halt of the siege artillery, during the march on Sikasso" (May 1898). From Méniaud, *Sikasso*, 89.

Why the Borrowings Matter 33

Figure 6. "A breach made in the walls of Sikasso by the artillery." From André Mévil, *Samory* (Paris: Ernest Flammarion, 1899), 197.

To quote the Malian historian Ibrahima Baba Kaké: "The taking of Sikasso was an event with incalculable consequences; in practical terms, it put an end to African resistance in West Africa. From that point on, the French faced only the unconquerable Samory, who in turn would be undone [*désarçonné*] a few months later." Samory surrendered to the French on September 29, 1898 and was sent into exile. It is said in Mali that "Tiéba and Samory served a third scoundrel [*larron*] by weakening each other mutually."[84] The French took Sikasso in order to clear the way for finally getting rid of Samory.[85]

The fall of Sikasso made the front page of the popular *Petit Parisien* on June 5, 1898, only a few weeks later (see Figure 8). Described as "an important military action" that has "just been accomplished," "the taking of Sikasso ... is an event of considerable importance for the definitive pacification of our possessions in West Africa. It will have the immediate effect of weakening what remains of Samory's power, now at the mercy of a decisive effort by our troops." Despite the dramatic cover art, the article is barely 500 words long; the "intrepid" enemy "Babemba, king of Canadougou" was to be "punished" for his "clearly hostile attitude."[86]

Figure 7. Illustration by Alpha Diallo, cover of *La Fin héroïque de Babemba, roi du Sikasso* by Cheikhou Oumar Diong (detail) (Dakar: Nouvelles Editions Africaines, 1980). Reprinted with the kind permission of Les Nouvelles Editions Africaines du Sénégal.

Figure 8. (opposite) "Nos soldats au Soudan: la prise de Sikasso, l'assaut final" (Our Soldiers in the Soudan: The Taking of Sikasso, the final assault), *Le Petit Parisien supplément littéraire illustré* 487, June 5, 1898. This engraving depicts the French side only in the battle of Sikasso: French officers (one falling) and the *tirailleurs sénégalais* fighting alongside them, depicted as steadfast and brave. Collection of the author. Scan by Hope & Feathers.

Vigné d'Octon called the defeat of Sikasso "the most abominable butchery to ever soil a French conquest."[87] French sources other than Vigné are virtually silent about any atrocities. But the Malian historian Soumaïla Sanoko confirms that "During the day of May 2, 1898, [Sikasso] was given over to pillage, under the complicit supervision of the officers of the column ... Many captives were sold on the spot, notably the women and children," and summary executions were numerous.[88] The historian (and President of Mali, 2003–08) Alpha Oumar Konaré reproduces a photograph, apparently taken by the French historian and eyewitness Jacques Méniaud, one which could serve as an illustration for the passage in question here: "The bodies of the populations that were fleeing"[89] (see Figures 9 and 10).

Konaré observes: "The Sikassois version of the taking of Sikasso has not yet been collected ... Since 1898 the families of Sikasso have been silent."[90] I want to suggest that Ouologuem, in his adaptation of the passage from Vigné, was working toward such local knowledge, filling in a crucial gap.

Figure 9. Cover of Alpha Oumar Konaré, *Sikasso Tata* (Bamako: Imprimeries du Mali, 1983).

Why the Borrowings Matter   37

Figure 10. "Les cadavres des populations en fuite" (The bodies of the fleeing population). Konaré, *Sikasso*, 61.

By borrowing this passage from Suret-Canale and/or Vigné d'Octon, without ever using the word Sikasso, Ouologuem invites us to think about this event of great importance in the history of his country and of West Africa in general. We should accept the invitation, cross the threshold, enter the portal, and ponder what it means. For one thing, this example on its own demonstrates the folly of separating textuality and history in any reading of *Le Devoir de violence*. By borrowing textually, Ouologuem delved into the historiography and, as we will see, altered it. It was *by borrowing text* that he invited us to think about something that he did not name: Sikasso and its role in history.

To return to the text(s): Suret-Canale (and Ouologuem after him) is quoting a French officer, who in turn is quoted in a work by Paul Vigné d'Octon, *La Gloire du sabre* (1900). Vigné stated: "I have in my possession a series of notes taken day by day, a sort of journal regularly maintained by an eyewitness. Here they are in all their terseness and distressing eloquence [*dans leur laconisme d'une navrante éloquence*]."[91] Vigné relies heavily on eyewitness accounts from French soldiers, most often unnamed. Here he goes on to quote from this journal, which is

38 *Thresholds*

marked "Sikasso, April 6, 1899" and signed "Lieutenant-commandant le Cercle, H...."

So as of now, we have at least four layers of voicing, of polyvocality. Working backwards chronologically:

1. Ouologuem's *Le Devoir*;

2. Suret-Canale's *Histoire*;

3. Vigné d'Octon's *La Gloire du sabre*;

4. The eyewitness "H." and his journal.

These form an archeological layering of embedded voices, all telling the same story. Or do they?

Not quite: Ouologuem, following his usual practice, did not simply copy and paste; he adapted. The artistry of his adaptations has often been ignored in discussions of his borrowings. Here, one word that he introduces would appear to have outsized importance: "mother." All the previous sources refer to the person who gives birth here as a "woman." Ouologuem alone attributes to her the status of mother, even as he goes on to describe how she is crushed by the onslaught of the fleeing crowd. The other details that he alone creates ("la mère hagarde qui boitille, délire, titube, vagissant, puis tombant") force us to see her suffering in all its horror; each of these words was carefully chosen to suggest a *via dolorosa*. In a book not known for its humanism, accused of "wallowing" in violence, Ouologuem goes beyond the "terseness" of his sources and restores the human condition of motherhood to a person who is being destroyed.[92]

Since Suret-Canale was quoting from Vigné, how can we know which book Ouologuem had in hand? We can't. But based on another borrowing from Vigné alone, we do know that Ouologuem used *La Gloire du sabre* as a source:

> Pourtant, à de très lointains intervalles, une caravane traverse l'étendue infinie et morne de ces plaines, caravane de négriers, le plus souvent poussant devant eux de lamentables théories d'hommes, de femmes, d'enfants couverts d'ulcères, étranglés par le carcan, mains ensanglantées par les liens. (*Le Devoir de violence*, 38)

> And yet, at infrequent intervals, a caravan traversed those dismal and endless plains: slave traders driving wretched files of men, women, and children, covered with open sores, choked in iron collars, their wrists shackled and bleeding. (*Bound to Violence*, 28)

This passage, which continues for another seven lines, is taken verbatim from *La Gloire du sabre* (3-4), and is not found in Suret-Canale.[93] For further context: Suret-Canale points out that the accusations made by Vigné d'Octon were never denied by the Ministry of Colonies, even when confronted about them in the Chamber of Deputies.[94]

Thinking about this woman and mother, in the first passage quoted above, as we are induced to do by Ouologuem, could take us deeper into the history of women in war in West Africa, and to the story of Ba Mousso Sano, wife of Tiéba and queen of Kénédougou, thus staying with the history of Sikasso. French imperialism liked to produce big books about travels and heroes and conquests, richly illustrated, designed to promote the empire. In one of these, devoted to Sikasso exclusively, Jacques Méniaud relates in glowing terms the story of Ba Mousso Sano, who reportedly surrendered her own child as a ritual sacrifice for her nation. Méniaud is full of praise for this act of sacrifice intended to help defeat Samory (in 1888), not the French (in 1899):

> Ba Mousso Sano is a *national heroine.* When Tiéba was informed, in 1887, that Samory was marching against him, there was great disquiet in Kénédougou. Tiéba did not lose hope of success ... he convoked the marabouts, who after palavers declared a very potent *gris-gris* would be necessary against so formidable an enemy. So that Allah would be favorable to Tiéba, it would be required to offer him one of the king's children. "Abraham did it and he was the chosen of God," they said.
>
> Tiéba hesitated, unable to decide in favor of a sacrifice that would remove one of his children from one of his wives. He spoke of his torment to Ba Mousso Sano, who said to him: "If it is to save you and to save your country, take my child."
>
> The first-born child of Ba Mousso Sano was thus killed [*immolé*] as an offering by the marabouts, and, in order to thank Ba Mousso Sano for her sacrifice, Tiéba swore that neither he nor anyone in Sikasso could ever say no to her, and that in all wars to come, her share [of the spoils] would be set aside.[95]

In his *Sikasso*, Méniaud honors Ba Mousso Sano with a stylized, art deco color illustration (see Figure 11), with the caption: "The wife of Tiéba offering her son to the sacrificing sorcerer for the salvation of Sikasso."[96]

The marabouts and Méniaud have lost track of the fact that Abraham in the end did not kill Isaac, after God let him off the hook. But tales of child sacrifice are not unknown, from Iphigenia (sacrificed by her father Agamemnon to appease the goddess Artemis) to Queen Pokou

Figure 11. Illustration by E. Charpentier, from Jacques Méniaud, *Les Pionniers du Soudan*, 2:322–23. Caption: "La femme de TIEBA offrant don fils au sorcier sacrificateur pour le salut de Sikasso" (The wife of Tiéba offering her son to the sacrificing sorcerer for the salvation of Sikasso).

Why the Borrowings Matter   41

of the Baoulé people, located close to Kénédougou in what is now Côte d'Ivoire.[97] The great Malian writer and contemporary of Ouologuem, Massa Makhan Diabaté, is one of the very few to depict Ba Mousso Sano, in his play *Une si belle leçon de patience*, calling her the "symbol of the city of Sikasso" and the incarnation of "our ancestral values." She narrates her own story in the play, giving her "express consent" to the sacrifice.[98] (Diabaté, always erudite, points out in a footnote that the etymology of Sikasso is "city of doubt.")[99] Inquiries among Malian friends and readings of Malian historians suggest to me that in the intervening years, Ba Mousso Sano has been forgotten.

What do these narratives have to do with *Le Devoir de violence*? There is no indication that Ouologuem was thinking about Ba Mousso Sano, although he must have heard of her. These stories have two things in common: Sikasso, and the death of a child: in one case, a victim of a war crime; in the other, a victim of a sacrifice. The textuality, intertextuality, borrowing, and adapting of texts have led us down this path to contemplate the fate of two babies, both dead, and their mothers: one horrifically destroyed, the other a queen remaining enthroned and revered. (Ba Mousso Sano survived the French conquest of 1898.)[100] They are women in war in Africa, with opposite fates. Much more could and should be said. I cite this as an example of how one borrowing in *Le Devoir de violence* can be a springboard for thinking about African history in all its complexity. While it might appear that this has taken us far from the text, I would argue that all of what I have reviewed here is packed into this one borrowing.

3. Borrowing in/and Translation

Since the first discovery of the borrowings   of the accused plagiarism—the question of translation has been danced around but not really examined. The Ouologuem scandal of 1972 erupted in the Anglophone world, starting with the *TLS*, based on passages from Graham Greene's *It's a Battlefield*. The infamous *TLS* exposé juxtaposed Ouologuem's French with Greene's original English, not its French translation, thus setting in motion an assumption that Ouologuem *translated as he borrowed*. But did he?[101]

There are four known Anglophone sources used in *Le Devoir de violence*: Greene's novel, James Baldwin's *Another Country*, John D. MacDonald's *The End of the Night*, and Raymond Chandler's *The Big Sleep*. Each existed in a French translation that was readily available in the mid-1960s, when Ouologuem was writing *Le Devoir*:

42 Thresholds

- *C'est un champ de bataille* by Greene, translated by Marcelle Sibon, had been in print since 1953;

- *Un autre pays* by Baldwin, translated by Jean Autret, was published in 1964;

- *Les Energumènes* by MacDonald, translated by Janine Hérisson, was published in 1962;

- *Le Grand Sommeil* by Chandler, translated by the famous writer and jazzman Boris Vian, was published in 1948.

From the beginning Anglophone critics (myself included) have assumed that Ouologuem translated and borrowed at the same time.[102] He knew English well and was certainly capable of doing so. But some French and Francophone critics have worked from the opposite premise: that Ouologuem borrowed from the existing French translations.[103] Which did he use?[104] We cannot know definitively, but we can do some forensic reading that might take us closer to an answer.

Two translators translating side by side will not always come up with the same translation. Take this beautiful sentence written by André Schwarz-Bart in response to the allegation that Ouologuem had plagiarized him: "Jamais livre n'en a gêné un autre."[105] I translated this as "One book has never stood in the way of another." Then I gave it to my husband, Christopher Rivers, who is a translator, and he came up with "Never has one book caused trouble for another." The verb *gêner* is particularly tricky and open to many choices in English, so this example is obvious. But surely, by examining some of Ouologuem's borrowings from English-language sources, we can get an educated hunch about which book he had in his hand.

I offer one example that seems to me convincing. Greene's original text reads:

> **"Everyone doing something different,"** she said, **her eyes going back to the double bed and her thoughts on the pink bedspread** in the other room and Jules and half a loaf is better than no bread and the lovely dead indifferent woman on the wall.[106]

Marcelle Sibon's translation:

> **"Ils font tous quelque chose de différent,"** dit-elle, tandis que ses yeux retournaient vers le grand lit, et **ses pensées vers la courtepointe rose dans** l'autre **chambre** et **vers** Jules, mais un demi-pain vaut mieux que pas du tout de pain, et que la ravissante et indifférente femme morte, dans son cadre.[107]

And *Le Devoir*:

> "**Ils font tous quelque chose de différent,**" murmura-t-elle, cependant que son regard revenait au grand lit, et **ses pensées vers la courtepointe rose, dans la chambre** de Chevalier, puis **vers** Saïf." (69)

"Bedspread" is a very generic term, whereas *courtepointe* is something much more specific, and a much less common term in French: a "counterpane" quilt; "counterpane" is Manheim's translation "back" into English (56). How likely is it that both Sibon and Ouologuem would have translated "bedspread" as "courtepointe"? Not likely, I think. What about "her dumb approval" (56), translated by both Sibon (88) and Ouologuem (68) as "la muette approbation de la jeune fille"? Not very likely. This is hardly a smoking gun, but I believe it indicates that, in this case at least—and probably with the other three Anglophone texts as well—Ouologuem was borrowing from the translation, not the original.

In the case of John D. MacDonald's *The End of the Night*, the sheer accumulation of identical choices makes it apparent that Ouologuem used the Hérisson translation: "a raunchy attitude" (130) in the original becomes "une attitude mesquine" in both the Hérisson[108] and the Ouologuem (130); MacDonald's "You're a swingin' thing, man. This is the William Tell bit" (134) becomes Hérisson's "Tu es épatant, mec. Nous allons jouer à Guillaume Tell" (170), almost identical to Ouologuem's "T'es épatant, mec. Nous allons jouer à Guillaume Tell" (132). And so on.

Other examples could no doubt be identified. This finding is open to different interpretations. If he was relying on existing French translations, it may suggest that Ouologuem was more confined to the Parisian literary world—and its choices about translations—than we have thought. In any case, if the borrowings are indeed portals of meaning, we need to know, to the extent that we can, which exact entrance Ouologuem was using: the English text or its French translation.

But there is an irony here: "no book has ever stood in the way of another," said the generous-minded Schwarz-Bart, but in fact Greene's *It's a Battlefield* and MacDonald's *The Edge of the Night* (actually *Les Energumès*, the Gallimard translation) not only stood in the way of *Le Devoir de violence*, they sank it. Because of the complaints made on behalf of Greene and MacDonald, Les Editions du Seuil threw Ouologuem under the bus and destroyed the reputation of his work, and his career. This happened even as Schwarz-Bart—who was much more

44   *Thresholds*

heavily borrowed from than any other living author—expressed support for Ouologuem and said that he was flattered.[109] Ouologuem returned to Mali in 1978 and regularly refused to see intrusive, unwanted would-be interviewers and scholars.[110] He died on October 14, 2017.

*

I have had little occasion here to comment on Ralph Manheim's translation, *Bound to Violence*, which is brutally vivid, deploying language that might be deemed unprintable now.[111] But critics have noticed aberrations in Manheim's work almost from its first appearance. This is a case of "unfaithful" translation, and I want to focus on one aspect of it that has not received attention. Critics have noted that Manheim added Anglophone literary allusions to his translation: short but famous quotations from T. S. Eliot and Emily Dickinson. But these allusions are worked into a long, elaborate *improvisation* invented by Manheim, which has not been discussed adequately.

In the middle of a scene of torture in *Le Devoir* that culminates in the execution of the French governor Vandame—a passage that Ouologuem largely borrowed from John D. MacDonald's *The End of Night/Les Energumènes* (see my table of borrowings)—Manheim inserted this improvisation of his own:

> "Oh, Governor," he [Kratonga] gasped. "I had such an awful dream. I dreamed about me. I thought some Whites were chasing me, and I couldn't run, and my neck was—oh, it was covered with blood. Oh-h, I can't go on."
>
> Vandame was seized with a panic terror, unreasoning, instinctive.
>
> "Not a soul need know what's happened to us," Kratonga wailed. And his dry, passionate talk commanded attention.
>
> For some time Vandame had not heard Wampoulo moving and had begun to wonder what he was doing.
>
> When he sensed danger, he groped at shapes and ran because he could not stop for death. Suddenly Wampoulo clasped his shoulders and shook them so frantically that Vandame's neck swung and broke.
>
> Quicker than speech, his arms waltzed above him, then rowed him softlier home, to the Artful Creator.
>
> Blood spurted from the nape of his neck like reluctant rubies grasped by a beetle. His eyeballs like frightened beads, Vandame drank a dewdrop from a blade of grass. He was a righteous man. (*Bound to Violence*, 115)

Why the Borrowings Matter **45**

The eye-catching phrase is, of course, he *could not stop for death*, which is a quotation from a poem by Emily Dickinson, "Because I Could Not Stop for Death."[112] We know that Ouologuem read and borrowed widely, but Emily Dickinson would be a new surprise. (In another part of the same passage, there is an allusion to Eliot's *The Waste Land*.)[113]

In fact, only the last sentence above was written by Ouologuem (and Schwarz-Bart before him): "C'était un juste." The rest is entirely of Manheim's (and Dickinson's) invention. It seems clear that Manheim went on a riff here, giving himself license to wax poetic, to indulge in alliteration ("reluctant rubies," "drank a dewdrop"), and to allude to Dickinson ("I Could Not Stop for Death"), no doubt with a wink to his readers. And what of this "Artful Creator" to whom one "rows" "softlier" home? This is not Ouologuem. The word *créateur* occurs only once in *Le Devoir de violence*, not in this passage; and there is no mention of him being "artful."

So there are two issues: on the one hand, as critic Joseph R. Slaughter puts it, "errant fragments of famous poetry written in English have wandered into the Manheim translation."[114] On the other, we have Manheim's own poetic riffs within a long improvised passage, at a key moment in the plot. Some truly bizarre textual play is going on here, in several layers: Ouologuem borrows from MacDonald and adapts the scene for an African context; Manheim translates while altering the scene and introducing his own and others' poetic conceits.[115]

Discussions of this passage go back to the first appearance of Manheim's translation. James Olney picked up on the discrepancy in the translation in 1976. (He did not know about MacDonald or any other borrowing except Greene.) He claimed in a footnote that Ouologuem had reviewed and corrected Manheim's entire translation; he was "assured" that that was the case, but he does not say by whom. It seems highly unlikely to me. Olney thought that Ouologuem himself introduced the allusion to Dickinson, but it seems clear to me that it was Manheim.[116] It is, however, worth pausing to consider that, if Olney were right and Ouologuem did review the translation and did introduce these Anglophone borrowings, the table of borrowings would have to be expanded to include them. Slaughter explored these added allusions in some depth in his essay "It's Good To Be Primitive," with an emphasis on copyright issues.

As A. N. Mensah rightly pointed out long ago, "the little echo of Emily Dickinson introduces feelings into that episode in the novel which are entirely out of place" (75). Did Manheim somehow get bored,

46   *Thresholds*

or repulsed by the violent cruelty of the scene, and decide to create a distraction by showing off his own literary skills, slipping in some poetry?

It is extraordinary—and highly inappropriate—for a modern translator to take such liberties, flying in the face of what Ruth Bush calls the "ethical responsibility" of the translator of postcolonial texts.[117] But this is unfortunately not without precedent among Western translators of Black literature, particularly in the early decades.[118] Are there other such improvised passages in *Bound to Violence*? I do not know. Did Manheim—one of the most prominent translators of the twentieth century, winner of a PEN award, a National Book Award for translation, and a MacArthur Fellowship—allow himself to add such cadenzas when he was working on *Mein Kampf*, or Céline's *Voyage au bout de la nuit*, or Brecht and Weil's *Threepenny Opera*, or the Freud/Jung letters, for that matter?

This discovery takes us beyond Ouologuem himself and reminds us that, despite his truly exceptional nature, he was not the only one with tricks up his sleeve. Manheim's improvisation is repeated in the 2023 Other Press edition (p. 152).

Ouologuem's Forgotten Farewell: "The World Is False"

It has been axiomatic among scholars of Ouologuem that he never explained himself after the accusations of plagiarism; not really; not fully or adequately. In his short "Polémique: *Le Devoir de violence*," published in *Le Figaro* on June 10, 1972, Ouologuem claimed, as we have seen, that his original manuscript had quotation marks surrounding the borrowed passages, suppressed by the publisher before publication. But that never made sense (if you put all those quotation marks back in, the text is incoherent). After that, retreat and silence: Ouologuem went back to Mali and renounced literature. As stated recently in the *New York Times*, "He never published again after the scandal."[119] While ignoring the four single-author books and the co-edited anthology that Ouologuem published after *Le Devoir de violence* (which is a considerable oversight), this narrative remains otherwise true, but with one important exception that has been completely overlooked.

In January of 1974, the magazine *Jeune Afrique* published a poetic essay by Ouologuem, "Le Monde est faux" (The World Is False).[120] It has been forgotten; no scholar of Ouologuem has mentioned it to my

Why the Borrowings Matter 47

Page 68
Dans ce beau texte
— dont Ouologuem a
bien voulu réserver la
primeur à
« Jeune Afrique » —
on n'aura pas de peine
à reconnaitre les
accents du « Devoir
de violence ».

Figure 12. Detail from table of contents, *Jeune Afrique*, no. 678/679, January 12, 1974. "In this fine text—which Ouologuem wanted *Jeune Afrique* to be the first to publish—the reader will have no trouble recognizing the tones of *Le Devoir de violence*."

knowledge, nor does it appear in any bibliography of his works (and yet it is listed in the MLA Bibliography, hiding in plain sight). In many ways it is the missing link: Ouologuem's explanation of what happened in France, how he got into a literary scandal, and why he returned to Mali. It is a remarkable document, part confession, part conversion narrative; a sort of mini-autobiography without names, dates, or places. In style, tone, and even content, this text resembles nothing so much as Fanon's chapter "L'Expérience vécue du Noir" in *Peau noire masques blancs*, the narrative of a consciousness that dilates and contracts as the world affects it. (I am not suggesting that there are borrowings.) This essay sheds new meaning on Ouologuem's literary trajectory: his rocket flight to success, and his fall, only to rise again, he suggests, in faith.

Addressed to an unknown "friend," the *inédit* is divided into four sections: "Toi qui es mon autre moi-même" (You Who Are My Alter Ego), "Savoir survivre" (Knowing How to Survive), "Un Infirme vainqueur" (An Unwell Conqueror), and "Une Odeur de mort" (An Odor of Death). Each section pivots back and forth between a "before" and an "after" and revolves around an idea of falsehood. The subject saying "I" here—let's call him Ouologuem—has had a revelation: he has discovered the falseness of the world and renounced it. One of the key terms is *désabusé*, disabused. The word itself suggests a prior condition of illusion or abuse, followed by a conversion to higher knowledge or insight: the very trajectory that Ouologuem describes here. He is battered by what he has been through; he is wounded:

> Lorsque la vie nous a tant soufflétés que, raides d'orgueil, nous ne sommes plus que la modeste ombre de nous face à nous-mêmes, et qu'alors, farouches comme la mort et plus solitaires qu'une lucidité désabusée,
> Nous n'avons de force autre que la force de murmurer: "Non."
> A quoi bon alors l'ami,
> A quoi bon se présenter désabusé à la face des hommes pour leur dire:

48 *Thresholds*

—Et voici mes blessures, et voilà mes plaies.

A quoi bon se présenter? Le monde est faux et marche sur le malentendu. (68)

When life has buffeted us so much that, stiffened with pride, we are nothing more than a modest shadow of ourselves looking at ourselves, then, fierce like death and more solitary than disabused lucidity,

We have only the strength to murmur: "No."

What good does it do at that point, friend,

What good does it do to present yourself, disabused, in the eyes of men, to say to them:

"Here are my wounds, and here are my scars."

What good does it do to present yourself? The world is false and works by way of misunderstandings.

These last lines (beginning "What good ...") are repeated throughout the piece like a refrain. It is impossible not to read this as Ouologuem's renunciation of his experience in France and its literary world, a world of illusions, appearances, and falseness. He renounces the education that led him into that world:

La course à l'instruction me rendit esclave de qui jugeait mon instruction, esclave de ma vanité d'instruit inquiétable par les notes, cette échelle mobile de l'intelligence abstraite. Alors je vis la fausseté de l'instruction et de la culture lorsque je vis que j'étais non pas producteur, mais consommateur et avaleur de bruits, puis débiteur de formules codées et folles comme des sonates célestes. (68)

The scramble for education made me a slave of those who judged my education, a slave of my vanity—the vanity of an educated person worried about grades, the sliding scale of abstract intelligence. Then I saw the falseness of education and culture, when I saw that I was not a producer but a consumer and swallower of noises, then a mere fountain of coded and crazy formulas like so many celestial sonatas.

That last sentence should perhaps not be taken literally as an allusion to the practice of literary borrowing ("a fountain of coded and crazy formulas"), but certainly it is relevant. And it is as close as Ouologuem comes to a confession of his literary transgressions. Everything here is a slightly veiled account of Ouologuem's experience; what is new to us now (since this piece seems to have been completely forgotten) is this unique statement about how it felt to him and how he has, at this point, changed his thinking and his life. What he did in the world of education and culture, he is telling us, was a *reaction* to the falseness of the world—not a creation of falsehood by him, which is what he was accused of. He implies that Paris was a hall of mirrors in which he was trapped.[121] His practice of literary trickery was merely a reflection of everything going on around him. Or so he seems to suggest. If the world is "a web of falsehoods" ("un tissu de faussetés"), then surreptitious literary borrowing is merely a reflection of that already false world. Ouologuem says that he "bought [himself] an Ariadne's thread" in the form of law dictionaries and works of Western literature. And:

> Alors, volé, trahi, trompé, vendu, je mis l'ordre que je pouvais dans mes affaires, et allai cesser d'agoniser chez les miens. (70)

> Then, robbed, betrayed, tricked, sold out, I put my affairs in order as best I could, and went home [among my people] to end my agony.

He is able to write this account because of a voyage of self-discovery ("Je descendis en moi-même"; I descended into myself), recounted in the simple past: "Et je vis combien la gifle du père était préférable aux malheurs de la vie" (And I saw to what an extent my father's slap was preferable to the miseries of life). Then comes the key moment of conversion: "Alors j'allais m'agenouiller à la face de Dieu" (So I went and knelt down before the face of God, 68). Later he says: "La fausseté du monde attendit. Et j'eus d'un coup, au frisson que je sentis à cette attente, la révélation du sentiment du sacré" (The falseness of the world was waiting. And all of a sudden I had, in the shivers that I felt from that waiting, the revelation of a sense of the sacred, 70). The future "Islamic militant"[122] that Ouologuem became is first revealed here, in 1974. Ouologuem is explaining his renunciation of the West and recounting his return to Africa, to family, and to faith.

Much more could be said about this dense piece. For the purposes of this book, it offers, *sotto voce*, Ouologuem's version of the events that we have seen, events about which so much has been written, from which his own voice was apparently missing (it was, in fact, waiting in the archive). That gap is now (re)closed. Without naming names, Ouologuem says how betrayed he felt, and how his actions had been those of a writer caught up in a world of falseness, which he has now renounced. When one thinks of all the scholars who, in later years, tracked him down and tried to get him to talk about his literary past, against his will, his rhetorical question resonates: "What good does it do to present yourself?"

50   *Thresholds*

Conclusion

All borrowing—all translation, all plagiarism—is the threshold of a portal from one text to another. Ouologuem, who so gleefully and masterfully practiced these arts, was shut down by those who, unlike Schwarz-Bart, did not want doors to be opened. The initial whistle-blower who wrote the sarcastically titled "Something *New* Out of Africa?" in the *TLS*, marking the beginning of Ouologuem's downfall, remains anonymous.[123]

Here we can pass through another portal: the "what if's" of this history. What if Ouologuem had not been so poorly treated by Seuil? What if he had defended his artistic practice more effectively?[124] What if, in a scholar's fantasy, Ouologuem had produced a completely annotated version of *Le Devoir de violence*, revealing all his sources and explaining his vision? (The 1974 "postscript" that I discussed is not that.) What if he had published the "history of contemporary Africa in several volumes" for which he signed a contract with Doubleday; or the "textbook on African history for American blacks" of which he spoke?[125] What if he had been allowed to further exercise his genius and to develop the plans he evidently had to advance education in Africa?[126]

In the decades since the Affaire Ouologuem and the disappearance of *Le Devoir de violence* from bookstores, a slow resuscitation of the novel has taken place. The publishing house Le Serpent à Plumes revived it in 2002. Sarah Burnautzki was the first scholar allowed to read—if not quote—the Ouologuem-Seuil files at the IMEC archive. Seuil itself brought *Le Devoir* back from oblivion in 2018—with a disingenuous, unsigned "note de l'éditeur."[127] In 2018 Jean-Pierre Orban changed the field of Ouologuem studies by revealing and reproducing documents that had previously been hidden, and by analyzing the entire complex publishing history revealed by items in the IMEC archive.[128] The current new wave of interest in Ouologuem, partly sparked by Mohamed Mbougar Sarr's novel *La Plus Secrète Mémoire des hommes*, which reimagines the Ouologuem story, is encouraging. Other Press republished the Manheim translation, *Bound to Violence*, in the fall of 2023.[129]

To make matters even more complicated, recent research by Professor Francine Kaufmann has revealed that changes were made to the text of *Le Devoir de violence* as it went through various printings in the fall of 1968. Were these changes made by Ouologuem himself? By the editors, with or without the author's knowledge? How extensive were they? What effect have they had, if any, on critics' work, even as no one realized that there were variants in different copies of the novel? Forthcoming work by Kaufmann and by Jean-Pierre Orban will take us a long way to answering these questions.

The number of borrowings in *Le Devoir de violence* may continue to expand as more are discovered. They are hiding in plain sight, right before our eyes. Those documented in my table and on Joël Bertrand's website can provide starting points for any number of inquiries into literary intertextuality and historical inquiry. As time goes by, artificial intelligence may help contribute to the list of borrowings.[130] Who knows what new paths Ouologuem will ultimately take us down?

Notes

1 My title is partly inspired by Sarah Burnautzki, "Yambo Ouologuem au seuil des Editions du Seuil," in *Fabula, les Colloques, L'œuvre de Yambo Ouologuem: un carrefour d'écritures (1968–2018)*, ed. Christine Le Quellec Cottier and Anthony Mangeon, 2019, https://www.fabula.org/colloques/document6018.php.
2 Matthieu Galey, "Un grand roman africain," *Le Monde*, October 12, 1968. See Christopher L. Miller, *Blank Darkness: Africanist Discourse in French* (Chicago: University of Chicago Press, 1985), 219; Yambo Ouologuem, *Le Devoir de violence* (Paris: Editions du Seuil, 1968), 14; trans. Ralph Manheim, *Bound to Violence* (London: Heinemann, 1971), 8. All references will be to this edition of the novel and its translation.
3 Ouologuem, quoted in Philippe Decraene, "Un Nègre à part entière," *Le Monde*, October 12, 1968.
4 Léopold Sédar Senghor, article in *Congo-Afrique* 33 (1969), quoted in Jean-Pierre Orban, "Livre culte, livre maudit: histoire du *Devoir de violence* de Yambo Ouologuem," *Continents manuscrits* (2018), http://journals.openedition.org/coma/1189.
5 I owe this analysis to Joël Bertrand, "*Le Devoir de violence* comme collage," https://joelbertrand.wordpress.com/436-2/. Consulted May 17, 2023. The English-language version is https://joelbertrand.wordpress.com/bound-to-violence-as-a-collage/ (henceforth referred to as Bertrand, "Collage").
6 "Something *New* Out of Africa?", *Times Literary Supplement*, May 2, 1972. This piece cites revelations made by Eric Sellin in his article "Ouologuem's Blueprint for *Le Devoir de violence*," *Research in African Literatures* 2, no. 2 (Autumn 1971): 117–20. Sellin discussed borrowings from Schwarz-Bart, not Greene; the *TLS* first revealed the passages from Greene.

52   *Thresholds*

7 Christopher Wise, "Introduction," in *Yambo Ouologuem: Postcolonial Writer, Islamic Militant*, ed. Christopher Wise (Boulder, CO: Lynne Rienner, 1999), 6.

8 The term *démarquage* (or *démarcage*) was used by the Seuil president Paul Flamand in his correspondence with Eric Sellin, quoted in Orban, "Livre culte, livre maudit," para. 111.

9 "Genital Reminders," *Times Literary Supplement*, 3486, December 19, 1968, emphasis added.

10 See Christopher L. Miller, *Impostors: Literary Hoaxes and Cultural Authenticity* (Chicago: University of Chicago Press, 2018).

11 Sarah Burnautzki made a similar argument about Africanization in her book *Les Frontières racialisées de la littérature française: contrôle au faciès et strategies de passage* (Paris: Honoré Champion, 2017), which I discuss below.

12 An early call to take the borrowings seriously, in an argument similar to the one I am making here, is found in Bernard Mouralis, "Un Carrefour d'écritures: *Le Devoir de violence* de Yambo Ouologuem," *Recherches et travaux: littératures africaines d'écriture française* 2, no. 27 (1984).

13 Joël Bertrand, "L'Intertextualité dans *Le Devoir de violence*," https://joelbertrand.wordpress.com/lintertextualite-dans-le-devoir-de-violence/.

14 Bertrand takes this term from Julia Kristeva, *Semiotike: recherches pour une sémanalyse* (Paris: Seuil, 1969), 332–33. Kristeva refers to *prélèvements* as "vestiges de livres désormais consommés et repris dans le texte," and says that "ces greffes jouent le rôle de ce que nous avons appelé un 'complexe signifiant.'"

15 Shaun F. D. Hughes, "Postcolonial Plagiarisms: Yambo Ouologuem, Calixthe Beyala, and Witi Ihimaera," *Forum for World Literature Studies* 3, no. 3 (December 2011): 386.

16 Souleymane Bachir Diagne, "1968: Crisis in African Letters," *Romanic Review* 101, nos 1–2 (January–March 2010): 150.

17 The Master's thesis by Antoine Habumukiza also identifies a number of sources for the first time (including Flaubert's *La Légende de Saint-Julien l'Hospitalier*) and offers excellent interpretations: Antoine Marie Zacharie Habumukiza, "*Le Devoir de violence* de Yambo Ouologuem: une lecture intertextuelle" (MA thesis, Queen's University, 2009). Over the years various critics have asserted that there are borrowings from Baudelaire, Georges Bataille, Zola, Proust, Hugo, Lautréamont, Ian Fleming, and perhaps others; none of these has been substantiated to my knowledge. The Qur'an is a special case. It is often cited as a source for Ouologuem, but to my knowledge there is no actual borrowing from the text. Christopher Wise mentions "echoes" of the Qur'an ("Ouologuem as Marabout Novelist," 187). See my table of borrowings with reference to p. 9 of the novel.

18 What Christine Chaulet-Achour wrote is completely true: "To merely identify Ouologuem's various sources and borrowings in *Bound to Violence* is not enough; we need to go further and ask ourselves what sort of relationships

the novelist seeks to establish with the diverse texts that he employs, reinscribing them into a new narrative configuration" (Christine Chaulet-Achour, "Writing as Exploratory Surgery in *Bound to Violence*," in *Yambo Ouologuem: Postcolonial Writer, Islamic Militant*, ed. Christopher Wise (Boulder, CO: Lynne Rienner, 1999), 100).

19 A reviewer of a book about the composer Olivier Messiaen comes up with a similar, if more elaborate comparison (which I found after writing about the borrowing of a car or a shovel), in order to make a different point: "If I borrowed my neighbour's lawnmower, for example, she would rightly expect it back after a specified time, but she would not expect me to have dismantled it, perhaps have made an air-compressor, or dry-ice maker out of the components, and added a set of curtains and some icing on top for good measure; she would want her lawnmower back." Robert Scholl, review of Yves Balmer, Thomas Lacôte, and Christopher Brent Murray, *Le Modèle et l'invention: Messiaen et la technique de l'emprunt*, review in *H-France* 23 (January 2023), no. 10. The reviewer's point is different from mine: he is focusing on the possible transformation of what is borrowed (what I call adaptation), while I am referring to confusion surrounding the concept of borrowing itself, as revealed in Posner's quote in my next sentence.

20 Richard A. Posner, *The Little Book of Plagiarism* (New York: Panirn Books, 2007), 11.

21 Another model that might be relevant here is the "cento verse" genre in classical Roman poetry, a patchwork poem made up entirely of borrowings. The difference is that such a poem would apparently lack the other dimensions that are so important in *Le Devoir*: adaptive language, paraphrase, and original writing. See https://poets.org/glossary/cento.

22 I am alluding to the French OULIPO (Ouvroir de littérature potentielle) group, founded in 1960, which was based on the idea of writing within self-imposed constraints. Its most famous production may be Georges Perec's novel *La Disparition*, which does not contain the letter "e."

23 On collage, see Bertrand, "Collage."

24 Achille Mbembe and Alain Mabanckou, "Plaidoyer pour une langue-monde: abolir les frontières du français," *La Revue du crieur* 2 (2018): 61–67.

25 "French Novelist Hits Back after MP Says She Must Show 'Greater Reserve,'" *Guardian*, November 13, 2009, https://www.theguardian.com/books/2009/nov/13/french-novelist-mp-reserve-goncourt. See Dominic Thomas, "The 'Marie NDiaye Affair' of the Coming of a Postcolonial *Evoluée*," in *Transnational French Studies: Postcolonialism and Littérature-Monde*, ed. Alec G. Hargreaves, Charles Forsdick, and David Murphy (Liverpool: Liverpool University Press, 2010), 146–63. Thomas writes: "the furore ... showed her to be trapped in a web of identity politics which, in the optic of the manifesto [on *littérature-monde*, 2007] had supposedly been consigned to the trash can of history" (146). See also Sarah Burnautzki, "L'Equivocité de

54 Thresholds

la visibilité de Marie NDiaye," in *Les Frontières racialisées de la littérature française. Contrôle au faciès et stratégies de passage* (Paris: Honoré Champion, 2017), 179–200.

26 See Alec G. Hargreaves, Nikki Hitchcott, and Dominic Thomas, eds, "Textual Ownership in Francophone African Literature," special issue, *Research in African Literatures* 37, no. 1 (Spring 2006).

27 See my *Impostors*, 74–76 and 90–104.

28 Dominic Thomas, *Black France: Colonialism, Immigration, and Transnationalism* (Bloomington: Indiana University Press, 2007), 83. For the broad context, see Ruth Bush, *Publishing in French: Literary Institutions and Decolonization, 1945–1967* (Liverpool: Liverpool University Press, 2016).

29 Thomas, *Black France*, 105.

30 Wilfried F. Feuser discussed similarities of theme and style between *Native Son* and *Le Docker noir*, without mentioning textual borrowing or plagiarism, in "Richard Wright's *Native Son* and Ousmane Sembene's *Le Docker noir*," *Komparatistische Hefte* 14 (1986): 103–16. Dominic Thomas took the analysis further, comparing passages of Sembene's novel and the French translation of Wright: *Black France*, 109–10. There are two other known cases of borrowing in Sembene's œuvre. His novel *O Pays mon beau peuple!* (Paris: Presses Pocket, 1957) is not only inspired by Jacques Roumain's *Gouverneurs de la rosée* (Port-au-Prince: Imprimerie de l'Etat, 1944); it reproduces certain passages of the Haitian novel. See Victor Aire, "Affinités électives ou imitation? *Gouverneurs de la rosée* et *O Pays, mon beau peuple!*", *Présence Francophone* 15 (1977): 3–10. The first accusation of plagiarism was made by Lamine Diakhaté and involved *Les Contes d'Amadou Koumba* by Birago Diop. See Diakaté, review of *Le Docker noir*, *Présence Africaine* 13 (1957): 153–54.

31 Pierre Assouline, "L'Affaire Beyala rebondit: l'Académie Française a pris le risque de cautionner un auteur dont l'œuvre est truffée de plagiats," *Lire* 252 (February 1997): 8–11.

32 Nikki Hitchcott, *Calixthe Beyala: Performances of Migration* (Liverpool: Liverpool University Press, 2006), 33. For a more recent overview, see Virginie François, "Une autrice prolifique et primée, malgré sa condamnation pour 'contrefaçon': Calixthe Beyala, l'effrontée du plagiat," *Le Monde*, August 4, 2021, https://www.lemonde.fr/series-d-ete/article/2021/08/04/calixthe-beyala-une-plagiaire-effrontee_6090549_3451060.html. See also Pius Adesanmi, "Strange Coincidences, Uncomfortable Influences: The Rage of Calixthe Beyela," *Glendora Review* 2, no. 1 (1997): 19–24.

33 On Beyala, see also Mireille Rosello, *Declining the Stereotype: Ethnicity and Representation in French Cultures* (Hanover: University Press of New England, 1998), especially her long note, at 187 n. 1. I disagree with Rosello's characterization of the term plagiarism as "invective" and its detection as a "blood sport." Plagiarism is both a legal term and a literary practice, and identifying it is no crime.

34 Andrée Blouin, *My Country, Africa* (New York: Praeger, 1983); Henri Lopes, *Le Lys et le flamboyant* (Paris: Seuil, 1997). See Ninon Chavoz, "Les dix petits nègres d'Henri Lopes," in *Henri Lopes: coups doubles*, ed. Anthony Mangeon (Paris: Sépia, 2021), 37–58; and Anthony Mangeon, "Henri Lopes au miroir d'Aragon," in Mangeon, *Crimes d'auteurs: de l'influence, du plagiat et de l'assassinat en littérature* (Paris: Hermann, 2016), 89–108.

35 Céline Gahungu, "Ramages: *Tribaliques* d'Henri Lopes," in *Henri Lopes: coups doubles*, ed. Anthony Mangeon (Paris: Sépia, 2021), 176–77; Gahungu, "A l'épreuve des pères: la phratrie congolaise," *Genesis: Manuscrits, Recherche, Invention* 51 (2020): 133. Sony Labou Tansi is also known to have borrowed from the French translations of *One Hundred Years of Solitude* and *Autumn of the Patriarch* by Gabriel Garcia Marquez: see Jean-Michel Devésa, *Sony Labou Tansi: écrivain de la honte et des rives magiques du Kongo* (Paris: L'Harmattan, 1996), 219–28.

36 The phrase "la phratrie des écrivains congolais" was coined by Sylvain Bemba in his article of that name: "La Phratrie des écrivains congolais," *Notre Librairie* 92–93 (March–May 1988): 13–15. See Alain Mabanckou, *Verre cassé* (Paris: Editions du Seuil, 2005).

37 The spirit in which this should be undertaken is best suggested by Ouologuem himself in his *Lettre à la France nègre* (Paris: Edmond Nalis, 1968), the passage I used as my epigraph.

38 See Miller, *Impostors*.

39 Francine Kaufmann is currently working on this subject.

40 Two efforts are worthy of note. Charles A. Larson, in his early publication, *The Novel in the Third World* (Washington, DC: Inscape, 1976), argues that the two novels display "two utterly different world views [...] representing opposing concepts of time and history" (47). His analysis is relatively short; the subject deserves a book-length study. Habumukiza also devotes a chapter to comparing the two novels on thematic terms ("*Le Devoir de violence* de Yambo Ouologucm," ch. 3).

41 This is Francine Kaufmann's paraphrase of accusations made by André Parinaud in *Paris-Journal* (October 28, 1959): Kaufmann, "Les enjeux de la polémique autour du premier best-seller français de la littérature de la Shoah," in *La Shoah dans la littérature française*, ed. Myriam Ruszniewski-Dahan and Georges Bensoussan, special issue, *Revue d'Histoire de la Shoah* 176 (September–December 2002): 68–96 (section 4). Kaufmann says: "L'accusation de plagiat fait long feu [...] *Le Mercure de France* dans son numéro de novembre 1959 signale que trois lignes sur la mort du rabbi de York sont empruntées à une lettre de Madame de Sévigné racontant l'exécution en 1676 d'une empoisonneuse (la Brinvilliers)." There were other instances of reproduction, but Kaufmann states that "most critics" put them in the category of normal historical research rather than plagiarism. For more information on the affair,

56   *Thresholds*

see Malka Marcovich, *La dernière rumeur du juste? Le miracle éditorial du Dernier des Justes d'André Schwarz-Bart* (Paris: Iggybook, 2020), 35–40.

42 Kaufmann, "Les enjeux," section 5.

43 Kaufmann, "Les enjeux," section 8.

44 It should be kept in mind that the effective end of both careers was not immediate. Schwarz-Bart went on to publish *La Mulâtresse Solitude* in 1972 and several works co-authored with Simone. Ouologuem remained (on and off, apparently) in France until 1978, co-edited a school manual in 1973 (see note 53 below), and published a second romance novel, *Le Secret des orchidées* (Paris: Editions du Dauphin, 1968, republished by Poche Select, Montreal, 1979). His essay published in *Jeune Afrique* in 1974, "Le Monde est faux," which I will analyze here, appears to be his farewell to France and literary life. It should also be noted that, in the discussion after my lecture at the ENS, Jean-Pierre Orban stated that Bertrand's table of borrowings from Schwarz-Bart is *not* complete, and that other borrowings (of as-yet-undetermined magnitude) from *Le Dernier des Justes* remain to be revealed. Professor Francine Kaufmann is expected to publish work on this soon.

45 I am grateful to Francine Kaufmann for an email of June 11, 2023 which allowed me to gain insight about the Schwarz-Bart Affair and its impact. André also collaborated with Simone on her multivolume *Hommage à la femme noire* (1988–89). After André's death in 2006, two co-authored novels were published: *Ancêtre en solitude* (2015) and *Adieu Bogota* (2017), one by him alone, *Etoile du matin* (2009), and a play.

46 Another, more complicated, comparison could be made to a writer with a highly vexed relationship to the Parisian literary establishment: Romain Gary/ Emile Ajar. The comparison was evoked when Ajar's *La Vie devant soi* won the Goncourt; see Marcovich, *La dernière rumeur*, 73. See also Miller, *Impostors*, 104–19.

47 André Schwarz-Bart, quoted in Orban, "Livre culte, livre maudit," para. 110. "J'ai toujours vu mes livres comme des pommiers, content qu'on mange de mes pommes, et content qu'on en prenne une, à l'occasion, pour la planter dans un autre sol."

48 Sarah Burnautzki, "Yambo Ouologuem au seuil des Editions du Seuil."

49 Quoted in Burnautzki, "Yambo Ouologuem au seuil des Editions du Seuil," para. 5.

50 V. Y. Mudimbe examined this trope in the work of Placide Tempels, the author of *La Philosophie bantoue*. See Mudimbe, *The Invention of Africa: Gnosis, Philosophy, and the African Order of Knowledge* (Bloomington: Indiana University Press, 1988), 53. And Homi Bhabha theorized the ambivalence of "colonial mimicry" in "Of Mimicry and Man: The Ambivalence of Colonial Discourse," *October* 28 (Spring 1984): 125–33.

51 Burnautzki writes in *Les Frontières racialisées de la littérature française*: "C'est en effet à partir de ces échanges [between Ouologuem and Seuil]

que la définition légitime d'une littérarité 'africaine' s'est négociée et ensuite concrétisée. De manuscrit en manuscrit, Yambo Ouologuem a donc 'africanisé' ses textes, ce qu'on lui avait en effet suggéré de faire dès les justifications de refus" (43).

52 Jean Cayrol, qtd. in Burnautzki, "Yambo Ouologuem au seuil des Editions du Seuil," para. 14.

53 Bastide, qtd. in Burnautzki, "Yambo Ouologuem au seuil des Editions du Seuil," para. 27.

54 Noémie Ndiaye, *Scripts of Blackness: Early Modern Performance Culture and the Making of Race* (Philadelphia: University of Pennsylvania Press, 2022), 8.

55 See the sections on Frobenius in Part Three of this study. And see V. Y. Mudimbe, *The Invention of Africa: Gnosis, Philosophy, and the Order of Knowledge* (Bloomington: Indiana University Press, 1988).

56 Walter D. Mignolo and Catherine E. Walsh, *On Decoloniality: Concepts, Analytics, Praxis* (Durham, NC: Duke University Press, 2018), 105.

57 See Blake Gopnik, "The Supreme Court May Force Us to Rethink 500 Years of Art," *New York Times*, March 1, 2023, https://www.nytimes.com/2023/03/01/arts/design/appropriation-warhol-renaissance-copyright.html?searchResultPosition=2#site-content; Colin Moynihan, "Why Warhol Images Are Making Museums Nervous," *New York Times*, March 6, 2023, https://www.nytimes.com/2023/03/01/arts/design/warhol-prince-goldsmith-museums.html?searchResultPosition=4. The Supreme Court's decision in *Andy Warhol Foundation for the Visual Arts v. Goldsmith* ruled that (quoting from the court's summary of Justice Sonia Sotomayor's majority opinion) "simply conveying 'a new meaning or message' through an artistically altered work was, on its own, 'not justification enough' to garner protection" (Matt Stevens, "After the Warhol Decision, Another Major Copyright Case Looms," *New York Times*, May 22, 2023, https://www.nytimes.com/2023/05/22/arts/warhol-prince-decision-copyright.html?searchResultPosition=1). This ruling thus directly targets an artistic practice like Ouologuem's. It must be said that there is nothing "simple" about creating "a new message or meaning." The Justices, in their ignorant hubris, thus belittle thousands of years of human creativity.

58 Richard Meyer, "The Supreme Court Is Wrong about Andy Warhol," *New York Times*, June 5, 2023, https://www.nytimes.com/2023/06/05/opinion/supreme-court-andy-warhol.html (emphasis added). See, among dozens of works on these interrelated subjects: Patrick Greaney, *Quotational Practices: Repeating the Future in Contemporary Art* (Minneapolis: University of Minnesota Press, 2014); Pierre Beylot, ed., *Emprunts et citations dans le champ artistique* (Paris: L'Harmattan, 2004); Akin Adeṣọkan, *Everything Is Sampled: Digital and Print Mediations in African Arts and Letters* (Bloomington: Indiana University Press, 2023). The following observation by Graham Huggan

58 Thresholds

is relevant: that *Le Devoir* is "a satire on origins, textual as well as cultural, for Ouologuem also takes every opportunity to violate the protective copyright of artistic originality"; "Anthropologists and Other Frauds," *Comparative Literature* 46, no. 2 (Spring 1994): 117. See also Diagne's remark that "The spirit of 1968 is about 'collages' and all sorts of subversion and appropriation of existing texts"; "1968: Crisis in African Letters," 151 n. 1.

59 Ahmadou Kourouma, *Les Soleils des indépendances* (Montreal: Presses de l'Université de Montréal, 1968/Paris: Editions du Seuil, 1970). See Patrick Corcoran and Jean-Francis Ekoungoun, "L'avant-texte des *Soleils des indépendances*," *Genesis* 33 (2011): 101, http://journals.openedition.org/genesis/616.

60 André Schwarz-Bart, *Le dernier des justes* (Paris: Seuil, 1959), 11.

61 André Schwarz-Bart, *The Last of the Just*, trans. Stephen Becker (New York: Atheneum, 1960), 3.

62 Yambo Ouologuem, *Le Devoir de violence* (Paris: Editions du Seuil, 1968), 9.

63 Ouologuem, *Bound to Violence*, trans. Manheim, 3. On "niggertrash": this horrible word can't be reproduced without comment. See my table of borrowings. There can be little doubt that Ouologuem picked up the word *négraille* from Aimé Césaire's masterpiece *Cahier d'un retour au pays natal*, which was well established as a key text in Black Francophone literature by the early 1960s. It appears 21 times in *Le Devoir de violence*, and the shocking, violent effect of the word was no doubt central to Ouologuem's intention in the novel. *Négraille* was also used by Fanon several times (see the table). The word appears in another of Ouologuem's source texts: Paul Vigné d'Octon, *La Gloire du sabre* (Paris: Société d'Editions Littéraires, 1900), 15. Ouologuem also used it in his *Lettre à la France nègre*, 168. The history of the word is murky because of its offensive nature; it is not found in the *Robert* dictionary, nor in the all-inclusive *Trésor de la langue française*. And it is "untranslatable." Translators of the *Cahier* have used a variety of formulas—from "nigger scum" (Clayton Eshleman and Annette Smith, trans., *The Collected Poetry of Aimé Césaire* (Berkeley: University of California Press, 1983), 37) to "the nigger cargo" (N. Gregson Davis, trans., *Journal of a Homecoming / Cahier d'un retour au pays natal* (Durham, NC: Duke University Press, 2017), 143). "Niggertrash" appears to be Manheim's own invention.

64 Manheim's translation reads: "died at forced labor, working for the colonials."

65 In email correspondence Joël Bertrand pointed out that "there is not a single Jewish character in *Le Devoir de violence*." There is nonetheless a debate to be had, since the Saïfs *claim* to be Jewish and are portrayed with extreme negativity.

66 See my commentary on *DV*, p. 12 in the table of borrowings. Hale finds the "portrayal of the rulers of Nakem as partially Jewish origin [...] plausible";

Thomas Hale, *Scribe, Griot, and Novelist: Narrative Interpreters of the Songhay Empire* (Gainesville: University of Florida Press, 1990), 150.

67 The phrase "the Jews of Africa" (or of any given country in Africa) is a trope of colonialism, one with which I believe Ouologuem is playing. To take just one example, Lieutenant-Colonel Monteil writes: "Beaucoup de Markas (branche de la race Bambara) se mélangent aux Senofos et exercent le commerce, ce sont les Juifs de la race noire." Parfait-Louis Monteil, *De Saint-Louis à Tripoli par le lac Tchad ... pendant les années 1890–91–92* (Paris: Félix Alcan, 1895), 43. This trope was very much alive in the then-Zaïre when I lived there in the mid-1970s; the Luba were referred to as the "Jews of Zaïre."

68 Hale, *Scribe, Griot, and Novelist*, 143.

69 Jean Suret-Canale, *Afrique Noire Occidentale et Centrale: géographie, civilisation, histoire*, 2nd ed. (Paris: Editions Sociales, 1961), 1:240; Chaulet-Achour, "Writing as Exploratory Surgery," 95–96.

70 Suret-Canale wrote an article about Vigné: "A propos de Vigné d'Octon: peut-on parler d'anticolonialisme avant 1914?", *Cahiers d'études africaines* 18, nos 69–70 (1978): 233–39. The answer is a qualified Yes, but only after 1911 in Vigné's case. Suret-Canale wrote that piece in response to Henri Brunschwig, "Vigné d'Octon et l'anticolonialisme sous la Troisième République (1871–1914)," *Cahiers d'études africaines* 54 (1974): 265–98. It is clear that Vigné—while opposed to the military "excesses" of colonialism and to its expansionism—held deeply racist ideas about Africans (274–75). Suret-Canale also wrote the introduction to another edition of *La Gloire du sabre* (Paris: Quintette, 1984). For some reason, this edition features shockingly racist (and gratuitous) illustrations.

71 See Diakité Madou and Sissoko Diomansi, *Le Royaume du Kénédougou et sa capitale Sikasso: contribution à la reconstitution de son histoire* (Bamako: Editions Jamana, 2014), 14, 21.

72 Gérard Brasseur, *Les Etablissements humains au Mali* (Dakar: Institut Fondamental d'Afrique Noire, 1968), 405.

73 See the lavish praise for Tiéba in Jacques Méniaud, *Les Pionniers du Soudan: avant, avec et après Archinard, 1879–1894* (Paris: Société des Publications Modernes, 1931), 1:564–65. One thing that Méniaud likes is that Tiéba is a "lukewarm Muslim, and tolerant." Méniaud was a lieutenant in the French army, *intendant de la colonne*, and thus a participant in the conquest of Sikasso. He says nothing of his own actions, but writes in the first person plural about the conquest. This is a classic case of history written by the winners. Writing in 1909, Collieaux, a colonial administrator, takes a revisionist view of Tiéba, referring to "ses passions sanguinaires de roi nègre." "Contribution à l'étude de l'histoire de l'ancien royaume de Kénédougou (1825–1898)," *Bulletin du Comité d'Etudes Historiques et Scientifiques de l'Afrique Occidentale Française* 1 (1924): 139.

60 *Thresholds*

74 See Yves Person, *Samori: la renaissance de l'empire mandingue* (Paris: ABC/ Dakar, Abidjan: NEA, 1976), 72–75.

75 For a granular analysis of the relations between France and Kénédougou during this period, see M. Tymowski, "The Rulers of Kenedugu (Tieba and Babemba) in the Face of French Colonial Expansion," in *Leadership and National Literature Movement in Africa*, ed. Thea Büttner, *Asia, Africa, Latin America* 7, special issue (Berlin: Akademie-Verlag, 1980): 37–46.

76 Tymowski, "Rulers of Kenedugu," 42.

77 Tymowski, "Rulers of Kenedugu," 43.

78 Bocar Cissé, "Babemba et la fin du Kénédougou," *Etudes Maliennes* 2 (May 1972): 33.

79 This more colorful version of the event is reported only by Alpha Oumar Konaré in *Sikasso Tata* (Bamako: Imprimeries du Mali, 1983), 50, without citation of a source (could this have been based on oral traditions made known to Konaré?). The quotations from Ba Bemba are reported by Méniaud (*Sikasso ou l'histoire dramatique d'un royaume noir au XIXe siècle* (Paris: F. Bouchy, 1936), 59), in the context of a full account of the negotiations between Morrison (who proposed establishing a permanent French presence in Sikasso, including *tirailleurs*) and Ba Bemba, who rejected that idea (Méniaud, *Sikasso*, 55–61). But Méniaud reports that, on his journey back to Bamako, Morrison was robbed and stripped (*Sikasso*, 60), not molested as Konaré reports. Another historian confirms the ambush and says Morrison's party was stripped "of its baggage, its uniforms, and its munitions": André Mévil, *Samory* (Paris: Ernest Flammarion, 1899), 193.

80 August Louis Charles Gatelet, *Histoire de la conquête du Soudan Français (1878–1899)* (Paris: Berger-Levrault, 1901), 399–400. Gatelet does not mention the molestation of Morrison, but says his party was attacked by "1,200 warriors." On Morrison's participation in the conquest, see p. 406. Gatelet's version of the death of Ba Bemba is that it happened in hand-to-hand combat, "où le fama et ses fidèles succombent glorieusement" (409).

81 Brasseur, *Les Etablissements humains*, 407.

82 Méniaud, *Sikasso*, 186: according to Méniaud, Ba Bemba ordered one of his own soldiers to shoot him, saying, "Ne me laisse pas tomber aux mains des Blancs." But Soumaïla Sanoko raises numerous doubts about this story; Ba Bemba may have simply died of wounds sustained in the battle. Soumaïla Sanoko, *Le Royaume du Kénédougou 1825–1898* (Bamako: Nouvelle Imprimerie Bamakoise, 2010), 185–87. Suret-Canale says that Ba Bemba got one of his soldiers to shoot him but was only wounded, then shot himself to death (*Afrique Noire*, 1:237).

83 Brasseur, *Les Etablissements humains*, 409.

84 Madou and Diomansi, *Le Royaume du Kénédougou*, 34.

85 This is stated by André Mévil (*Samory*, 187–88).

86 "Nos Soldats au Soudan," *Le Petit Parisien supplément littéraire illustré* 487, June 5, 1898, 182–83.

87 Vigné, *La Gloire du sabre* (Paris: Société d'Editions Littéraires, 1900), 130.

88 Sanoko, *Le Royaume du Kénédougou*, 188.

89 Méniaud, *Sikasso*, 61.

90 Konaré, *Sikasso*, 58, 68.

91 Vigné, *La Gloire du sabre*, 131.

92 This case could be taken as an example of the larger, "interstitial" phenomenon described by Bacary Sarr in "Du *Devoir de violence* à *Peuls*: quand Yambo Ouologuem et Thierno Monénembo explorent les interstices de la mémoire colonial," *Fabula* (2019), https://www.fabula.org/colloques/document6024.php. Sarr writes: "L'on peut constater d'emblée à quel point les deux romans se fondent sur une mise en scène de la subversion et une rhétorique déviante pour bousculer et débusquer les silences et les secrets de l'histoire coloniale occultés" (para. 15).

93 The use of the word *théorie* in this passage inspired the title of my second book, *Theories of Africans: Francophone Literature and Anthropology in Africa* (Chicago: University of Chicago Press, 1990). I thought I was quoting from Ouologuem alone, but it was in fact Vigné through Ouologuem. I do not believe that this borrowing has been previously identified.

94 Suret-Canale, *Afrique noire*, 1:245.

95 Méniaud, *Les Pionniers du Soudan*, 2:322–23. See Sanoko, *Le Royaume du Kénédougou*, 187. Konaré (*Sikasso*, 44) reproduces many photographs of the conquest, which he attributes to Méniaud; some of these photos (not the horrific ones) are found in Méniaud's *Sikasso*.

96 Méniaud, *Sikasso*, facing p. 104; see text on 193. An American dissertation reports Ba Mousso Sano's sacrifice of her child as fact, citing only Méniaud: Levell Holmes, "Tieba Traore, Fama of Kenedougou: Two Decades of Political Development" (diss., University of California, Berkeley, 1977), 301. Holmes writes: "Jacques Méniaud's momentous collection and documentation of the French military history in the Sudan supplies the most accurate and extensive references to Tieba and Kenedougou" (22). Collieaux reports a different sacrifice: a blood price had to be paid by one of the members of Tiéba's family, but it was one of his brothers, Tiémorotoma, who volunteered to be killed by throwing himself into battle with the enemy ("Contribution à l'étude," 143–44).

97 In the discussion after my lecture, Catherine Mazauric suggested a comparison to the Baoulé queen Abraha Pokou, who, around 1770, was said to have sacrificed her only son, throwing him into the Comoé River "in order to save her people." See Véronique Tadjo, *Reine Pokou, concerto pour un sacrifice* (Paris: Actes Sud, 2004), 7. Tadjo calls this a "legend." See also Jean-Noël Loucou and Françoise Ligier, *La Reine Pokou, fondatrice du royaume Baoulé* (Paris: ABC, 1977). I owe the allusion to Iphigenia to

62   Thresholds

Joël Bertrand. On infanticide, see Mary-Kay F. Miller, *(Re)productions: Autobiography, Colonialism, and Infanticide* (New York: Peter Lang, 2003).
98 Massa Makhan Diabaté, *Une si belle leçon de patience* (Paris: ORTF-DAEC, 1972), 81.
99 Diabaté, *Une si belle leçon de patience*, 48 n.: "Sika (doute), so (maison, village, ville), d'où Sikasso: la ville du doute." Konaré gives several alternatives coming from various languages, including village of the horse, of couscous, and, most widely accepted, village of the elephant (*Sikasso*, 13).
100 Sanoko, *Le Royaume du Kénédougou*, 194: "Le premier grand personnage qui fit sa soumission fut la célèbre veuve de Tiéba, Bamousso Sanou. Elle s'installa en dehors de la cité murée, sur l'autre rive du Lotio, dans un quartier qui portera désormais son nom, *Sanoubougou* (hameau de Sanou)." There is a neighborhood with a market in Sikasso called Sanubugu or Sanoubougou. Alpha Oumar Konaré makes no mention of the child sacrifice in his *Sikasso*. Collieaux reports that Tiéba had "around 400" wives and Ba Bemba "around 500" ("Contribution à l'étude," 173); he makes no mention of Ba Mousso Sano.
101 Greene and his publishers initially wondered how the passage from *It's a Battlefield* "got through" the French translation and into Ouologuem's novel. Alan Hill, the head of Heinemann Educational Books, said that when he received word of the borrowing, from Graham Greene himself, "I immediately turned up [*sic*] the pages and there it was. It was remarkable how *it has survived in translation*." Quoted in James Currey, *Africa Writes Back: The African Writers Series & the Launch of African Literature* (Oxford: James Currey, 2008), 68, emphasis added. Currey writes: "An Australian research student in Zambia had told Graham Greene that he had spotted that Yambo Ouologuem had transferred the words *in the French translation of this novel* from a Dover boarding house into a similar seedy setting in Africa" (68, emphasis added). How an Australian living in Zambia had procured the French translation, *C'est un champ de bataille*, is a bit mysterious.
102 Tobias Warner's brilliant essay is based on this premise: "Bodies and Tongues: Alternative Modes of Translation in Francophone African Literature," in *Traces 4: Translation, Biopolitics, Colonial Difference*, ed. Naoki Sakai and Jon Solomon (Hong Kong: Hong Kong University Press, 2006): "The Graham Greene passages ignited the controversy and censorship because they were an incident of plagiarism-as-translation" (311).
103 See, for example, Habumukiza's analysis of the Sibon translation of Greene ("*Le Devoir de violence* de Yambo Ouologuem," 83ff.).
104 I have only seen one critic address this question, long ago: Robert McDonald, "*Bound to Violence*: A Case of Plagiarism," *Transition* 41 (1972): 64–68. McDonald was not able to obtain the French translations in question (66). He concludes with an Orwellian question which exactly echoes the predicament of the protagonist writer in Sembene Ousmane's *Le Docker noir*:

"M. Ouologuem has no possible way of proving conclusively that he *did* write his book" (68).

105 André Schwarz-Bart, letter to François-Régis Bastide (Lausanne, August 16, 1968) qtd. in Orban, "Livre culte, livre maudit," para. 120.

106 Graham Greene, *It's a Battlefield* (London: William Heinemann, 1934), 57.

107 Graham Greene, *C'est un champ de bataille*, trans. Marcelle Sibon (Paris: Robert Laffont, 1953), 90.

108 John MacDonald, *Les Energumènes*, trans. Janine Hérisson (Paris: Gallimard, Série Noire, 1962), 166.

109 For a full account of how this all happened, see Orban, "Livre culte, livre maudit." Seuil continued to sell copies until 1982, then stopped production for 36 years. The English translation remained in print until 2003. The narrative arc of Ouologuem's fall from grace is complicated, and his writings are more extensive than is generally known. Just after *Le Devoir*, he published, under the name Utto Rodolph, the erotic novel *Les Mille et une bibles du sexe*, "with a preface by Yambo Ouologuem" (Paris: Editions du Dauphin, 1969). Before the scandal he published a romance novel under the name Nelly Brigitta, *Les Moissons de l'amour* (Paris: Editions du Dauphin, 1970); and after, under the same name, *Le Secret des orchidées* (Montreal: Presses Select, 1979). He began another novel called *Les Pèlerins du Carpharnaüm*, some pages of which remain at the IMEC archive. See Orban, "Livre culte, livre maudit."

110 See Christopher Wise, "In Search of Yambo Ouologuem," in *Yambo Ouologuem: Postcolonial Writer, Islamic Militant*, ed. Christopher Wise (Boulder, CO: Lynne Rienner, 1999), 199–218.

111 In the 2023 Other Press edition, Manheim's language is not bowdlerized; it remains the same.

112 A. N. Mensah, "Yambo Ouologuem's *Bound to Violence*: A Reconsideration of a Prize-Winning Novel," *Universitas: An Inter-Faculty Quarterly* 1, no. 3 (new series) (March 1972): 75–80. The poem in question is one of Dickinson's most famous, "Because I Could Not Stop for Death."

113 See Joseph R. Slaughter, "'It's Good to Be Primitive': African Allusion and the Modernist Fetish of Authenticity," in *Modernism & Copyright*, ed. Paul K. Saint-Amour (Oxford: Oxford University Press, 2011), 285–86.

114 Slaughter, "It's Good to Be Primitive," 285.

115 Yet another twist—beyond what I can account for here—comes from Slaughter, who found fragments of "Frank Norris's classic novel of lust, greed, and murder in late nineteenth-century San Francisco" (*McTeague: A Story of San Francisco* (New York: Doubleday, Page, 1914)) in Manheim's translation, but not in the original. See Slaughter, "It's Good to Be Primitive," 289. (The novel appears to have been translated into French, as *Les Rapaces*, only in 2012.) So this seems to suggest that Manheim was not just an improvisor and an enthusiast of allusions; he was also a borrower, like Ouologuem.

64   *Thresholds*

116 James Olney, *Tell Me Africa: An Approach to African Literature* (Princeton: Princeton University Press, 1973), 234 n. 19. Olney says: "I am assured that Ouologuem himself rewrote the passage after the translation was done," but he does not identify his source. I think it is highly unlikely that Ouologuem did that. Olney also seems to be the first to have recognized allusions to T. S. Eliot's *The Waste Land* and *Four Quartets* in *Bound to Violence*. Writing after Olney, Charles Larson adds other information that complicates the whole question: "Olney wrote to Ouologuem's translator, Ralph Manheim, and learned from him that Ouologuem rewrote a number of the passages in the English version of the novel"; Larson, *Novel in the Third World*, 53. Larson here footnotes Olney's *Tell Me Africa*, 208, where Olney does *not* mention this. Olney says elliptically, in the passive voice: "*I am assured* that Ouologuem himself rewrote the passage after the translation was done and that he made several other small changes after reading the translation" (234, emphasis added). This is all very confusing. If Olney learned from Manheim that Ouologuem reviewed and edited the translation, why did he not say this himself in *Tell Me Africa*? If Ouologuem reviewed the translation, did he really approve changes that radically altered the scene in question? And allow Manheim to improvise about some "Artful Creator" and such things? It seems unlikely. I owe the seed of my own belated "discovery" of this problem to an article that has apparently been forgotten, and wrongly so. Published in 1972 (but with no reference to borrowing or plagiarism), A. N. Mensah's "Yambo Ouologuem's *Bound to Violence*: A Reconsideration of a Prize-Winning Novel" is a negative review of the novel, which Mensah finds "sensationalist," and of the translation, which he finds lacking (although he has not read the French original). Mensah realized that there was something strange about the allusion to Dickinson; he wondered how this bit of Dickinson got into Ouologuem's novel—how would it have been rendered in French, and how did it get "back" to English?

117 Bush, *Publishing in French*, 182.

118 Ruth Bush cites Femi Ojo-Ade's critique of John Reed's "mangled" translation of Ferdinand Oyono's *Une vie de boy* (*Publishing in French*, 183). And there were problems in the first translation of Camara Laye's *L'Enfant noir* by James Kirkup and Ernest Jones (*The Dark Child* (New York: Farrar, Strauss and Giroux, 1954)). See Miller, *Theories of Africans*, 135 n. 31. The first translations of Frantz Fanon's works were notoriously awful. Christopher Wise's translation of this passage in *Le Devoir* of course does not contain Manheim's inventions: *The Yambo Ouologuem Reader: The Duty of Violence, A Black Ghostwriter's Letter to France, and A Thousand and One Bibles of Sex*, trans. and ed. Christopher Wise (Trenton: Africa World Press, 2008), 135.

119 Ben Libman, "A Novel Reconsiders an African Writer Tarnished by Scandal," *New York Times*, September 26, 2023, https://www.nytimes.com/2023/09/26/books/review/mohamed-mbougar-sarr-most-secret-memory-of-men.html. If the scandal began on May 5, 1972 with the publication of

the unsigned article "Something *New* Out of Africa?" in the *Times Literary Supplement*, it would be hard to say when the scandal "ended."

120 Yambo Ouologuem, "Le Monde est faux: inédit," *Jeune Afrique* 678/679 (January 12, 1974): 68–70. The essay is announced on the front page of the magazine and is accompanied by a drawing by the Egyptian artist George Bahgory. See Christopher L. Miller, "Ouologuem's Forgotten Farewell: 'The World is False,'" *Continents manuscrits* [Online], HS 2018, Online since 19 December 2023, connection on 20 December 2023. URL: http://journals.openedition.org/coma/11324.

121 Ouologuem's representation of (unnamed) Paris thus echoes the image of the metropole in Ousmane Socé's *Mirages de Paris* (Paris: Nouvelles Editions Latines, 1937). See Christopher L. Miller, "Hallucinations of France and Africa," in *Nationalists and Nomads: Essays on Francophone African Literature and Culture* (Chicago: University of Chicago Press, 1998), 55–89.

122 See Wise, *Yambo Ouologuem.*

123 "Something *New* Out of Africa?", *TLS*, May 5, 1972. It was *TLS* policy at the time for all reviews to appear unsigned; many have been identified in the intervening years, but not this one. See my letter to *TLS*, September 2, 2022; https://www.the-tls.co.uk/articles/shakespeares-private-life/.

124 Ouologuem's assertion that Seuil had suppressed quotation marks in his manuscript has never seemed credible; if such marks were inserted in the novel, they would be ubiquitous and make no sense, unless they were accompanied by footnotes. No original manuscript has been found. See Ouologuem, letter to editor, *Le Figaro littéraire*, June 10, 1972; and see my *Blank Darkness*, 223–25.

125 Orban, "Livre culte, livre maudit," para. 76. On the textbook, see Penelope McMullen, "Where the Oppressors Are Black," *Newsday*, Nassau edition, March 11, 1971, 98.

126 See Yambo Ouologuem, R. Pageard, and M. T. Demidoff, *Introduction aux lettres africaines* (Paris: Editions de l'Ecole, 1973). In the introduction to this *manuel scolaire*, Ouologuem says "ce premier ouvrage n'est donc qu'un premier pas vers une culture ouverte au champ des possibles."

127 Yambo Ouologuem, *Le Devoir de violence* (Paris: Seuil, 2008).

128 Orban, "Livre culte, livre maudit."

129 Yambo Ouologuem, *Bound to Violence*, trans. Ralph Manheim, ed. with annotations by Chérif Keïta (New York: Other Press, 2023).

130 As of now, I am somewhat skeptical about the contributions of artificial intelligence. Until such time as all works of literature are digitized, much remains out of reach of even the most powerful engines. The goal of total completion remains asymptotic. My skepticism about bots increased when I entered an unidentified quotation from *Le Devoir* into Chat.OpenAI on August 28, 2023. The quotation is "Le Saint-Père n'approuve guère le café au lait" (p. 19), and the context makes clear that racial mixing is being discussed. The first time I asked, the bot confidently told me that the sentence came

66   *Thresholds*

"from the French author Gustave Flaubert's novel *Madame Bovary*. It can be found in Part Two, Chapter Nine of the novel." This is not true: it is not in that chapter nor anywhere else in *Madame Bovary*. (I searched a PDF and reread the chapter itself.) I asked again, and, like a Magic 8 Ball, the bot came up with a different answer: it is "attributed to Pope Pius X": "Pope Pius X reportedly expressed this disapproval of coffee with milk, suggesting that he preferred his coffee black. However, it's worth noting that this statement is often shared humorously and may not be a direct quote from Pope Pius X himself. It has become a part of cultural anecdotes and conversations related to coffee preferences." Asked a third time, the bot confessed: "I apologize for any confusion earlier. The phrase 'Le Saint-Père n'approuve guère le café au lait' is actually a humorous and fictional line from the French novel *Bonjour Tristesse* written by Françoise Sagan. The novel was published in 1954. The line has been misattributed to Pope Pius X in various contexts, but its actual origin is within the pages of this novel." So I got a digital edition of *Bonjour Tristesse*, thinking that it would indeed make a likely source for Ouologuem. The quotation does not appear in that novel. I asked the bot what chapter it was in, and it again confessed, even more embarrassed this time: "I apologize for any confusion, but it appears that there might be a misunderstanding. After further research, I couldn't find any specific reference to the phrase 'Le Saint-Père n'approuve guère le café au lait' in the novel *Bonjour Tristesse* by Françoise Sagan. It's possible that there might be confusion or misinformation regarding the origin of this phrase." Confusion and misinformation, indeed.

PART THREE

The Borrowings in Yambo Ouologuem's *Le Devoir de violence*:

A "Complete" Table

- Words in boldface are identical from one text (the source) to the other (*Le Devoir de violence*). Many others are close paraphrases of the source's language. I have not marked those.

- I have counted as "identical" words that are the same but of different form (tense, number, gender, etc.).

- This table is intended to be a schematic summary. It makes reference to every instance of borrowing of which I am aware, but it does not reproduce every borrowed word.

- In cases of extensive borrowing (Schwarz-Bart, Maupassant), I have given examples.

- For a table of borrowings that includes complete, unabridged quotations, see Joel Bertrand, "*Le Devoir de violence* comme collage." English-language version: https://joelbertrand.wordpress.com/bound-to-violence-as-a-collage/

- For full bibliographical information about all sources, see both the list of principal sources below and the notes preceding the table.

- Principal Works Cited:

  o Bertrand, Joël. "*Le Devoir de violence* comme collage." The annexes of this paper contain the most complete information available about

68 Thresholds

the borrowings in *Le Devoir de violence*: https://joelbertrand.
wordpress.com/436-2/.

o Chaulet-Achour, Christine. "Writing as Exploratory Surgery in
Bound to Violence," in *Yambo Ouologuem: Postcolonial Writer,
Islamic Militant*, ed. Christopher Wise (Boulder, CO: Lynne Rienner,
1999), 89–108.

o Habumukiza, Antoine Marie Zacharie. "*Le Devoir de violence* de
Yambo Ouologuem: une lecture intertextuelle." MA thesis, Queen's
University, 2009.

o Orban, Jean-Pierre. "Livre culte, livre maudit: histoire du *Devoir
de violence* de Yambo Ouologuem," *Continents manuscrits*, 2018.
http://journals.openedition.org/coma/1189.

o Wise, Christopher, ed. *Yambo Ouologuem: Postcolonial Writer,
Islamic Militant* (Boulder, CO: Lynne Rienner, 1999).

LE DEVOIR DE VIOLENCE	HYPOTEXT OR	SCHOLARLY SOURCES AND
(Paris: Seuil, 1968). The version referred to here is marked on the back cover "Imprimé en France 9-68.7." On the last page of the novel, there is the code: D.L. 3e TR. 1968 No. 2187-7 (5018). The meaning of this code remains to be determined. The first printing was marked: Imp. Aubin, à Liguge (Vienne) D.L. 3e Tr. 1968 No. 2187 (4743). Forthcoming research by Professor Francine Kaufmann reveals that the version I am using includes changes that were made after the initial printing in September. This table does not take those variants into account. This version was the basis of all further reprints of the novel.	SOURCE TEXT	COMMENTS

A "Complete" Table   69

The novel begins as a parody or pastiche of *Le Dernier des Justes*. These borrowings are too extensive to be reproduced in their entirety here; examples follow. See Bertrand for full documentation.

André Schwarz-Bart, *Le Dernier des Justes* (Paris: Seuil, 1959). This novel, which won the Prix Goncourt, tells the saga of a Jewish family from the Middle Ages to the Nazi era. Each generation has one *juste*, the last of whom dies in an extermination camp.

These are the best-known and most notorious of all of Ouologuem's borrowings. Note the heavy use of paraphrase (here and throughout the novel): "boivent" for "reçoivent," "soleil" for "étoiles," "première moitié" instead of "deuxième quart," etc.

Numerous sources have documented and analyzed the relation between *Le Devoir de violence* (*DV*) and *Le Dernier des Justes*. Eric Sellin, "Ouologuem's Blueprint" was one of the first (in 1971). His article contains precise quotations comparing Schwarz-Bart to Ouologuem.

Example 1 (p. 9)
The opening of the novel.
"**Nos yeux** boivent l'éclat du soleil ... **tiendrait aisément dans** la première moitié de ce **siècle; mais la véritable histoire** des Nègres **commence** beaucoup, beaucoup plus **tôt**, avec les Saïfs, **en l'an** 1202 **de notre ère, dans** l'Empire africain de Nakem, au Sud du Fezzan, bien après les conquêtes d'Okba ben Nafi el Fitri."

Example 1 (p. 11)
"**Nos yeux** reçoivent la lumière d'étoiles mortes. Une biographie de mon ami Ernie **tiendrait aisément dans** le deuxième quart du XXe **siècle; mais la véritable histoire** d'Ernie Lévy commence très tôt, **vers l'an** mille **de notre ère, dans** la cité anglicane de York. Plus précisément: le 11 mars 1185."

For the most complete documentation of these borrowings, see Bertrand, Annexe 3. Bertrand shows 26 borrowed passages, lettered from A to Z.

In the discussion after my lecture at the ENS, Jean-Pierre Orban stated that Bertrand's table of borrowings from Schwarz-Bart is not complete, and that other borrowings (of as-yet-undetermined magnitude) from *Le Dernier des Justes* remain to be revealed.

Example 2 (p. 10)
"Mais ce récit ne présente **rien de** frappant."

The following passage makes a similar gesture: "Raconter la splendeur de cet empire—dont la renommée, atteignant le Maroc, le Soudan, l'Egypte, l'Abyssinie, la noble et sainte ville de la Mecque, fut connue des Anglais, des Hollandais, des Français, des Espagnols, des Italiens, et, bien entendu, des Portugais—**n'offrirait rien** que du menu folklore."

Example 2 (p. 12)
"Cette anecdote n'offre **rien de** remarquable en soi."

Christine Chaulet-Achour, "Writing as Exploratory Surgery in *Bound to Violence*, in *Yambo Ouologuem, Postcolonial Writer, Islamic Militant*, ed. Christopher Wise, 90–93, contains numerous comparative quotations.

Antoine Habumukiza's MA thesis, "*Le Devoir de violence* de Yambo Ouologuem: une lecture intertextuelle" appears to be the most comprehensive accounting and cataloguing of intertextuality in *DV* to be produced in an academic context. It is indispensable for our purposes. It is surpassed in volume only by Joël Bertrand's website.

70 Thresholds

Example 3 (p. 11)
"**Ici, nous atteignons** le degré critique au-delà duquel la tradition se perd dans la **légende, et s'y engloutit; car** les récits écrits font défaut, et les versions des Anciens **divergent** de celles des griots, lesquelles s'opposent à celles des **chroniqueurs.**"

Example 3 (p. 13)
"**Ici, nous atteignons** le point où l'histoire s'enfonce dans la **légende et s'y engloutit; car** les données précieuses manquent, et les avis des **chroniqueurs divergent.**"

Habumukiza's third chapter is a comparative reading of the two novels in thematic terms. His work recommends itself not only for its careful cataloguing of intertextuality in *DV*, but also for its sharp analysis.

Orban makes a very important remark: it is astonishing that no one at Seuil (which had published *Le Dernier des Justes*) noticed the resemblances, as obvious as they are ("Livre culte, livre maudit," para. 118). It is all the more surprising—as Schwarz-Bart himself pointed out in a letter to François-Régis Bastide—in that the same editor, Bastide, handled both books. But see Schwarz-Bart's own reaction, quoted in Orban (para. 120): "Ce qui me gêne, vois-tu, ce qui m'offense, c'est ton mutisme tout au long de l'élaboration de ce travail." At the same time, Schwarz-Bart was adamant and constant in his argument that his books were "apple trees" from which anyone was free to pick the fruit, and that "jamais livre n'en a gêné un autre."

Example 4 (pp. 14, 16)
"**Véridique ou** fabulée, la légende de Saïf Isaac el Heït hante de nos jours encore le romantisme nègre [...] **Il fallut se rendre à l'évidence:** l'eau de la sainte Mecque ne lui gagna aucun ami, ne rendit guère la vue aux aveugles, ne **guérit** point les paralytiques et même— sacrilège!—n'avait pas, aux dires des mécréants, bon gout ..."

Example 4 (p. 14)
"**Véridique ou** trompeuse, la vision de Salomon Lévy suscite l'intérêt général [...] **Mais il fallut se rendre à l'évidence:** ses mains ne **guérissaient** pas les plaies, ses yeux ne versaient aucun baume ..."

In Example 4, Ouologuem comes close to making a thesis statement for the novel's revisionist, anti-Negritude, anti-establishment stance. That he does this while writing a parody of Schwarz-Bart— thereby setting up a parallel between the history of the Europeans and that of Africans— makes this an astonishing writerly *tour de force.*

Borrowings from *Le Dernier des Justes*, as documented by Bertrand, Habumukiza, and others, continue up to p. 35 in *DV* ("Comment, pénétré de déplaisir ..."), then stop, with only two more to come, in the final dialogue of the novel, on p. 207 ("SAIF: Jouez! Heureux les politiques ...") and in the final paragraph of the novel, pp. 207–08.

A "Complete" Table   71

p. 9 The interjections in Arabic that open the novel and continue throughout: "*Maschallah! oua bismillah! ... oualahi! ...*"	See translations in Christopher Wise, "Ouologuem as Marabout Novelist," in Wise, ed. *Yambo Ouologuem: Postcolonial Writer, Islamic Militant*, 186ff. Thomas Hale calls these "asides to God," and points out that they punctuate the narration of the entire novel. Hale, *Scribe, Griot, and Novelist*, 155.	Wise writes: "*Bismillah* [literally, "In the name of God" ...] is the opening line of every sura (but one) in the Qur'an" (*Yambo Ouologuem*, 186). This invocation occurs four times in the novel, on pp. 9, 23, 61, and 207. I have not counted this as a borrowing because, while it occurs many times in the Qur'an, it is also a common every day expression ("an invocation used by Muslims at the beginning of any undertaking" according to the Oxford Dictionary), and therefore not specific to the Qur'an.
p. 10 "Il en fut ainsi à Tillabéri-Bentia, à Granta, à Grosso, à Gagol-Gosso, et dans maints lieux dont parlent le *Tarik el Fetach* et le *Tarik el Sudan* des historiens arabes."		For Ouologuem's adaptations "from the content and the form" of Songhay chronicles, including the *Tarikh el-Fettach* and the *Tarikh es-Soudan* see Thomas Hale, *Scribe, Griot and Novelist*, ch. 8. No actual textual borrowings are cited. Hale does not offer a page-by-page analysis, but he provides examples. On the names of peoples as reworked by Ouologuem (e.g. Randé for Mande), see *Scribe, Griot and Novelist*, 139. On the relation of *DV* to epic, see also Repinecz, who calls *DV* a "notorious antiepic" which "relentlessly and harshly satirizes the epic tradition" (Jonathon Repinecz, *Subversive Traditions: Reinventing the West African Epic* [East Lansing: Michigan State University Press, 2019], 37).

72 Thresholds

---

p. 11

"Ainsi, Saïf Moché Gabbaï de Honaïne—sur les dires d'un devin, lequel lui avait prédit en 1420, un jour d'entre les jours, qu'il serait renversé par un enfant à naître dans l'année en cours, à Tillabéri-Bentia, capitale de l'Empire nakem [...] fit goûter la mort rouge à tous les nouveau-nés, dont il aligna les têtes réduites le long du mur de son antichambre. Mais—de loin plus fortunée que combien d'autres!—une mère, Tiébirama, sauva son nouveau-né à la faveur de la nuit, fuyant, suivie de son époux et de trois serviteurs fidèles, pour s'installer à Gagol-Gosso."

Habumukiza compares this to the Gospel According to Matthew, 2:13–23, the flight of the Holy Family into Egypt after King Herod's decree.

---

p. 12

Maurice Delafosse, *Haut-Sénégal-Niger* (Paris: Maisonneuve et Larose, 1972 [1912]), 1:211.

See Repinecz, *Subversive Traditions*, Figure 5, p. 57, which juxtaposes this passage from *DV* with two excerpts from Maurice Delafosse (1870–1926), the French colonial administrator and ethnologist. Repinecz's table demonstrates that Ouologuem was certainly influenced by Delafosse and targeting his theory for satire; but actual textual reproduction is limited to place names, making this a case of borrowing that is very different from, for example, the use of Suret-Canale.

"Le Seigneur—saint est Son Nom—nous a accordé la faveur de faire apparaître, à l'origine de l'Empire nègre Nakem, la splendeur d'un seul, notre ancêtre le **Juif** noir Abraham El Heït, métis né d'un père nègre et d'une mère juive d'Orient—de Kénana (Chanaan)—**descendant** des Juifs de **Cyrénaïque** et du Touat, qu'une migration secondaire à travers l'Aïr aurait porté au Nakem, selon l'itinéraire de Cornélius Balbus."

"Mais vers 320 avant J.-C. à la suite de la prise de Jérusalem par Ptolémée Soter, de nombreux **Juifs** furent déportés en **Cyrénaïque**. Sans doute ils y trouvèrent, plus ou moins mélangés d'éléments berbères, les **descendants**, devenus nombreux et puissants, des fractions israélites ou hyksos venues d'Egypte longtemps auparavant, et il se forma là une population fort importante, d'origine judéo-syrienne dans son ensemble et pratiquant des religions diverses qui, toutes,

In the second passage from Delafosse quoted by Repinecz, which I do not reproduce here, the terms **Kénana** (**Chanaan** ...), **Cyrénaïque**, **Touat**, and **Bornou** are all found.

Repinecz offers "a new interpretation of the *Devoir*'s intertextuality" (53); that the vision of history in the novel "cannot be fully appreciated unless we read it

A "Complete" Table   73

	devaient dériver plus ou moins du culte des Hébreux primitifs ou culte d'Abraham. C'est à cette population que je crois pouvoir faire remonter l'origine ethnique des Peuls ou du moins de celles de leurs fractions qui n'ont pas été trop transformées par des unions avec des Noirs."	intertextually through Delafosse" (54). Habumukiza also discusses the shadow of Delafosse in *DV* (108). Repinecz refers to Delafosse's theory of "a great Judeo-Syrian migration across Africa" as "invention" and as a "monstrous brainchild on the basis of actual genealogical traditions" (58). It was thus ripe for Ouologuem's take-down. Habumukiza, for his part, compares this same passage to Genesis 12–25, Abraham's flight into Canaan—as an allusion. "Cornelius Balbus" is presumably Lucius Cornelius Balbus, a wealthy Roman consul and friend of Julius Caesar. He kept a diary, but it was lost. It is not clear what Ouologuem is referring to as his "itinéraire" (which, like *voyage* in French, can mean both a journey and a literary account of it).
pp. 12–13	Flaubert, "La Légende de Saint Julien l'Hospitalier," in *Trois contes* (Paris : Garnier-Flammarion, 1965), 105.	Habumukiza, 75. On 76, examples of plagiarism. On 77, an example of transformation.
"Enfin: l'Eternel bénit Isaac: **des esclaves en fuite, des** paysans **révoltés, des** braves gens **sans fortune, des** guerriers, des aventuriers, des orphelins, **toutes sortes d'intrépides affluèrent sous son drapeau,** lui *composant* une armée. **Elle grossit. Il devint fameux. On le recherchait."**	**"Des esclaves en fuite, des** manants **révoltés, des** bâtards **sans fortune, toutes sortes d'intrépides affluèrent sous son drapeau,** et il se *composa* une armée. **Elle grossit. Il devint fameux. On le recherchait."**	
p. 14 "Mort en 1490, Saïf Isaac el Héït, le doux et juste empereur, laissa trois fils: l'aîné de tous, Josué, sacrifié à Dieu; le puîné Saïf El Haram; le cadet Saïf El Hilal"		Habumukiza (66–67) compares this passage to Genesis 9:18–27, the story of Noah and his sons.

74   *Thresholds*

p. 19 (in English) "(a demi-Moor in his proper colour, bound with a cord.)"	This is quoted from the description of the coat of arms of the notorious British slave trader John Hawkins.	I did not include this in the list of author-sources.
p. 19 "Le Saint-Père n'approuve guère le café au lait …"	Unknown source. See my note about searching for this with a chatbot.	
p. 22 "Afrique fantôme"	Title of a book by Michel Leiris: *Afrique fantôme* (Paris: Gallimard, 1934).	
Beginning on p. 9, occurrences of the term *négraille*, a rare and offensive word most likely borrowed from Césaire. The word is used 21 times in *DV*; it could be argued that the shocking, violent effect of the word was central to Ouologuem's tonal intention in the novel, hence the frequency of its use : • 9 (in the third sentence) • 18 (twice) • 29 • 31 • 41 • 44 • 81 • 82 • 101 • 111 (twice) • 136 • 137 (twice) • 138 • 143 • 178 • 189 (twice) • 191	Aimé Césaire, *Cahier d'un retour au pays natal* (first published in *Volontés*, 20 [1939]: 23–51), used several times, most famously at the key moment of uprising on a slave ship: "Et elle est debout la négraille." Ouologuem would have known the word from reading Césaire. But it should be noted that Frantz Fanon also used the word: twice in *Peau noire, masques blancs* (Paris: Seuil, 1952), 20 and 89; and once in *Les Damnés de la terre* (Paris: François Maspero, 1978 [1961]), 153.	The *Encyclopedia Britannica* wrongly states that Ouologuem "coined" this term. The word was in circulation at least since the nineteenth century, as its occurrence in the Corbière novel demonstrates. But it was given currency in the twentieth century by Césaire, from whose *Cahier* Ouologuem no doubt picked it up. Translators of the *Cahier* have used a variety of formulas—from "nigger scum" (Clayton Eshleman and Annette Smith, trans., *The Collected Poetry of Aimé Césaire* (Berkeley: University of California Press, 1983), 37, to "the nigger cargo" (N. Gregson Davis, trans., *Journal of a Homecoming / Cahier d'un retour au pays natal* (Durham, NC: Duke University Press, 2017), 143. "Niggertrash" appears to be Manheim's own invention.

	This offensive word is not in the *Robert* dictionary, understandably. For that matter, the definitive *Trésor de la langue française* does not include it either. But the French Wiktionary cites a novel about the French slave trade: Edouard Corbière, *Le Négrier, aventures de mer* (Paris: Dénain et Delamare, 1834 [1832]), 3: 154. « que ça n'aille pas plus loin, que toute la négraille m'appelle *Monsieur le Marquis* [...] (See Miller, *The French Atlantic Triangle*). The word also appears (cited ironically as reported speech) in another of Ouologuem's source texts: Paul Vigné d'Octon, *La Gloire du sabre* (Paris: Société d'Editions Littéraires, 6th edition, 1900), 15. This work is discussed below.	
The title of Part Two: "L'extase et l'agonie."	A play on the title of Irving Stone's biographical novel about Michelangelo, *The Agony and the Ecstasy* (1961). Translated by Janine Michel as *Puissant et solitaire, la vie ardente de Michel-Ange* (Paris: Presses de la Cité, 1962).	This case of borrowing from an Anglophone work differs from others in that Ouologuem clearly used the English original title rather than the French translation.

76   Thresholds

p. 37

"Tout est pris, saccagé, volé—et les captifs, au nombre de huit mille environ, sont rassemblés en un troupeau dont le colonel commence la distribution. Il écrivait lui-même sur un calepin, puis y renonçait, clamant: 'Partagez-vous cela!'
Et chaque Blanc obtint plus de dix femmes noires à son choix. Retour au quartier général en étapes de quarante kilomètres avec les captifs. Enfants, malades ou invalides: tués à coups de crosse et de baïonnette. Et leurs cadavres, laissés au bord de la route. Une femme est trouvée accroupie. Elle est enceinte. On la pousse, on la bouscule à coups de genoux. Elle accouche debout en marchant. A peine coupé le cordon et jeté, d'un coup de pied, hors de la route, l'enfant, l'on avance, sans s'inquiéter de la mère hagarde qui boitille, délire, titube, vagissant, puis tombant, cent mètres plus loin, écrasée par la foule.

[...]

Jean Suret-Canale, *Afrique Noire Occidentale et Centrale*, 1:240.

"Tout est pris ou tué. Tous les captifs, 4000 environ, rassemblés en troupeau. Le colonel commence la distribution. Il écrivait lui-même sur un calepin, puis il y renonce en disant: 'Partagez-vous cela.' Le partage a lieu avec dispute et coups. Puis, en route! Chaque Européen a reçu une femme à son choix ... On a fait au retour des étapes de quarante kilomètres avec ces captifs. Les enfants et tous ceux qui sont fatigués sont tués à coups de crosse et de baïonnette ... [ellipsis in original]
Les cadavres étaient laissés au bord des routes. Une femme est trouvée accroupie. Elle est enceinte. On la pousse à coups de crosse. Elle accouche debout en marchant. A coupé le cordon et abandonné l'enfant sans se retourner pour voir si c'était garçon ou fille.

Chaulet-Achour, "Writing as Exploratory Surgery," 97–98. This is a very interesting case. It seems to be the only case in which Ouologuem borrowed from a modern historian. But the layering of discourse is actually much more complex than that.

In this passage, Suret-Canale is describing, in vivid and horrifying terms, the conquest of the city of Sikasso (in what is now Mali) by French forces on May 1, 1898.

For full documentation, see Bertrand, Annexe 4.X.

But the words reproduced here are not Suret-Canale's. (Chaulet-Achour overlooked a footnote.) Suret-Canale (and Ouologuem after him) is quoting a French officer, who in turn is quoted in a work by Paul Vigné d'Octon, *La Gloire du sabre*, 130ff. It was revived in 2006 with a preface by Abdelaziz Bouteflika (President of Algeria, 1999–2019) by the Algiers-based Editions ANEP, and appeared in a series called "Voix de l'anticolonialisme." (Chaulet-Achour did not follow Suret-Canale's footnote leading to Vigné d'Octon.)

For this passage, Ouologuem could have had either book— Suret-Canale's or Vigné d'Octon's—in hand. Vigné "d'Octon"—a nom de plume— (1859–1943), a medical doctor, deputy in the National Assembly, and ubiquitous colonial and "antico-lonial" writer (author of works like *Au Pays des fétiches* and *Terre de mort: Soudan et Dahomey*), also published numerous novels, one of which won the prize of the Académie Française.

Les Nègres réquisitionnés en route pour porter le mil restent cinq jours sans rations; reçoivent quarante coups de cravache s'ils prélèvent une poignée des dix à vingt-cinq kilos de vivres qu'ils portent sur leurs têtes nues, rasées. Les tirailleurs, le commun des soldats, les sous-officiers et officiers ont tant d'esclaves qu'il leur est impossible de les compter, les loger ou les nourrir."

Dans ces mêmes étapes, les hommes réquisitionnés en route pour porter le mil restent cinq jours sans rations; reçoivent cinquante **coups de corde s'ils prennent une** poignée de mil qu'ils portent.

Les tirailleurs ont eu tellement de captifs qu'il leur était impossible de les loger et de les nourrir."

Suret-Canale wrote an article about Vigné: "A propos de Vigné d'Octon: peut-on parler d'anticolonialisme avant 1914?", *Cahiers d'études africaines* 18, nos 69–70 (1978): 233–39. The answer is a qualified Yes, but only after 1911 in Vigné's case.

Suret-Canale wrote that piece in response to Henri Brunschwig, "Vigné d'Octon et l'anticolonialisme sous la Troisième République (1871–1914)," *Cahiers d'études africaines* 54 (1974): 265–98. It is clear that Vigné— while opposed to the military "excesses" of colonialism and to its expansionism—held deeply racist ideas about Africans; see Brunschwig, "Vigné d'Octon," 274–75.

Chauet-Achour calls this a case of "implicit quoting" (95). I would say that it is more than that; it qualifies as plagiarism. It is also a fascinating case of triply indirect speech, chaneling the original "voice" of an (unnamed) French officer who took contemporaneous notes.

Vigné writes: "Je possède une série de notes prises au jour le jour, une sorte de journal régulièrement tenu par un témoin occulaire. Les voici dans leur laconisme d'une navrante éloquence" (97–98). So there are four archeological levels of voicing and textuality here: the officer, Vigné d'Octon, Suret-Canale, and finally Ouologuem. Vigné relies heavily on eyewitness accounts from French soldiers, most often unnamed.

See the commentary in the body of my essay.

78   *Thresholds*

p. 38

"Pourtant, à de très lointains intervalles, une caravane traverse l'étendue infinie et morne de ces plaines, caravane de négriers, le plus souvent poussant devant eux de lamentables théories d'hommes, de femmes, d'enfants couverts d'ulcères, étranglés par le carcan, mains ensanglantées par les liens.

En vols serrés, corbeaux, charognards, vautours chauves au long cou pelé la suivent, certains qu'à chacune de ses étapes, ils auront, pour se repaître, les cadavres de ceux ou de celles qui, affaiblis par leurs blessures, ou les entrailles ravagées par la famine, succomberont; et ceux aussi qu'on abandonnera vivants sur la route, parce que leurs pieds, rongés jusqu'aux os par les plaies et la fatigue, refuseront de les porter ..."

The borrowing from Vigné, *La Gloire du sabre* continues: pp. 20–21.

"Pourtant, à de très lointains intervalles, une caravane traverse l'étendue infinie et morne de ces plaines, caravane de négriers le plus souvent poussant devant eux de lamentables théories d'hommes, de femmes, d'enfants couverts d'ulcères, étranglés par le carcan, mains ensanglantées par les liens.

En vols serrés, corbeaux, charognards, vautours chauves au long cou pelé la suivent, certains qu'à chacune de ses étapes ils auront, pour se repaître, les cadavres de ceux ou de celles qui, affaiblis par leurs blessures, ou les entrailles ravagées par la famine, succomberont; et ceux aussi qu'on abandonnera vivants sur la route, parce que leurs pieds, rongés jusqu'aux os par les plaies et la fatigue, refuseront de les porter plus avant.

To my knowledge this borrowing has not been identified previously. I cited this passage from *DV* in my book *Theories of Africans*, whose title was inspired by it. At the time I had no idea that the passage was borrowed.

This passage comes from Vigné (*La Gloire du sabre*, 3-4) but is not found in Suret-Canale, proving that Ouologuem borrowed directly from the former; he may have used Suret-Canale as well (for the passage quoted above), we don't know.

Ouologuem changed the punctuation slightly, adding several commas and a semicolon. He left out Vigné's last two words and encased the passage with ellipses, which may hint at the borrowing.

There is another possible intertextual dimension here, although it does not involve borrowing. The siege and conquest of Sikasso is told from an unabashedly pro-colonial French point of view by Jacques Méniaud in *Sikasso ou l'histoire dramatique d'un royaume noir au XIXe siècle*, a richly illustrated text which recounts the battle from a technical and triumphalist standpoint.

The passage in Méniaud that corresponds to the events recounted by Vigné, Suret-Canale, and Ouologuem is the following:

A "Complete" Table 79

pp. 38–39
"Dans tout le Haut-Randé, ainsi que dans le Yamé, au nord et au sud du Grand Fleuve, de Krotti-Bentia à Dangabiara, il n'y a ni route ni sentier qui ne soient jalonnés de nombreuses étapes pareilles, gîtes de mort et de crime, dépôts résiduels du seul commerce qui fleurisse en ces contrées, sous la protection de l'homme blanc ... De l'avis de tous les gens de bonne foi qui ont vu ces pays et qui y vécurent, une caravane d'esclaves dits de guerre, qu'elle soit dirigée par les indigènes ou pas, laisse sur sa route le tiers environ de sa cargaison de chair humaine, avant d'arriver, soit au marché où se fera la vente, soit au poste où aura lieu la distribution."

pp. 21–22
"Dans tout le Haut-Sénégal, ainsi que dans la bouche du Niger, au nord et au sud du grand fleuve, de Koulikoro à Tombouctou et Bandiagara, il n'y a pas de routes ni de sentiers qui ne soient marqués de nombreuses étapes pareilles, gîtes de mort et de crime, dépôts résiduaire du seul commerce qui fleurisse en ces contrées sous la protection de notre drapeau. Ainsi que je le démontre plus loin, de l'avis de tous les hommes de bonne foi qui ont vu ces pays et qui y vécurent, une caravane d'esclaves dits de guerre, qu'elle soit dirigée par des indigènes ou par nos troupes, laisse sur sa route, pour les causes que je viens de dire, le tiers environ de sa cargaison de chair humaine avant d'arriver soit au marché où se fera la vente, soit au poste français où aura lieu la distribution."

"De 7 h. à 9 h. du matin, plus de 5.000 guerriers abandonnaient ainsi la défense intérieure, entraînant à leur suite et protégeant des groups de population civile, hommes, femmes, enfant chargés des fardeaux les plus variés. "Les spahis ne cessent de harceler les fuyards. Vers 9 h., ils chargent une troupe de cavaliers puis enveloppent un convoy d'habitants escorté de 300 sofas qui déposent leurs armes. *Spectacle magnifique*: les officiers en tête, la troupe alignée comme au champ de manœuvre, *les spahis galopent, sabrent, font des prisonniers*, traversent des marais apparemment infranchissables, ne connaissent aucun obstacle" (179, emphasis added).

It is not hard to fill in the gaps in this text with the horrors that were recounted by the unknown officer, then by Vigné, and repeated by Suret-Canale and Ouologuem.

* Bertrand discovered this borrowing.

80   *Thresholds*

p. 43 The story of Prince Aniaba, including the quote "Prince Aniaba; il n'y donc plus de différence entre vous et moi que du noir au blanc." Attributed to Louis XIV.	Versions of the story of Aniaba appear in various sources. The quote from Louis XIV is found in Paul Roussier, *L'Etablissement d'Issiny 1687–1702* (Paris: Larose, 1935), xxiii. Roussier writes: "C'est sans doute à cette époque que Louis XIV dit en riant à son filleul [Aniaba] le mot que rapporte le liturgiste Claude Chatelain: 'Prince Aniaba, il n'y a donc plus de différence entre vous et moy que du noir au blanc …'"	See my *Blank Darkness: Africanist Discourse in French* (Chicago: University of Chicago Press, 1985), 32–33.
p. 52 "Alors il la vit […] regard allumé."	Bertrand compares this to a passage in *Les Mille et Une Nuits*, "Ibrahim et Gamila."	Bertrand, Annexe 4.XVII.
p. 52	Guy de Maupassant, "Marroca," in *Contes et nouvelles* (Paris : Gallimard, 1974) 1:370–71. First of two uses of this story in *DV*.	Bertrand, Annexe 4.III.
"Aux environs, **personne. Rien qui remuât. Pas un cri d'oiseau,** nul chant de cigale, **pas un bruit, pas même un clapotement, tant** le fleuve **immobile** semblait **engourdi sous le soleil. Mais dans l'air cuisant,** Kassoumi **croyait saisir une sorte de bourdonnement de feu.**"	"**Personne dehors; rien ne remuait; pas un cri** de bête, un vol d'oiseau, **pas un bruit, pas même un clapotement, tant** la mer **immobile** paraissait **engourdie sous le soleil. Mais dans l'air cuisant,** je **croyais saisir une sorte de bourdonnement de feu.**"	
p. 54 The borrowings from this story by Maupassant continue, ending with: "**Le lendemain,** qui était un vendredi, Kassoumi revint. **Elle était encore au bain,** la coquine! **mais**: tout habillée cette fois."	"Je revins **le lendemain. Elle était encore au bain, mais** vêtue d'un costume entier."	

A *"Complete"* Table   81

pp. 55–56	Baldwin, *Un Autre pays*, trans. Jean Autret (Paris: Gallimard, 1964), 38.	Joël Bertrand was the first to discover this significant use of Baldwin, the only African American writer whose work was borrowed in *DV*. Bertrand quotes the larger context, Annexe 2. I reproduce here only the section which contains textual borrowing.
"La femme portait l'homme comme la mer un navire, d'un mouvement lent de bercement, avec des montées et des descentes, suggérant à peine la violence sous-jacente. Ils murmuraient, sanglotaient au cours de ce voyage, et leurs mouvements, avec insistance, s'accélérèrent au point de devenir d'une puissance insoutenable, et qui fusait d'eux. L'homme poussa un grognement, laissant aller son arme plus vite, plus loin, plus fort entre les cuisses de la femme. Le venin jaillit; et soudain ils sentirent qu'ils manquaient d'air, qu'ils allaient exploser ou mourir! Ce fut une seconde d'un bonheur suraigu, idéal et charnel—affolant."	"Leona le **portait**, comme la **mer** porte un bateau, **d'un mouvement lent de bercement, avec des montées et des descentes, suggérant à peine la violence sous-jacente. Ils murmuraient** et **sanglotaient au cours de ce voyage**, et lui, doucement, mais avec insistance, il jurait. Chacun s'efforçait d'atteindre un port. Il ne pourrait pas y avoir de repos tant que ce mouvement ne serait pas **accéléré, au point de devenir insoutenable, par la puissance** qui surgissait en **eux**. Rufus ouvrit les yeux un moment et regarda le visage de la femme, transfiguré par une joie délirante, qui luisait dans le noir comme de l'albâtre. Des larmes s'attardaient au coin de ses yeux, et ses cheveux étaient moites près du front. Elle respirait avec des gémissements et de petits cris, disait des mots qu'il ne pouvait comprendre, et, malgré lui, il commença à aller plus vite, et plus loin. Il voulait qu'elle se souvienne de lui, jusqu'à la mort. Et rien ne put l'arrêter	In the text of *DV* quoted here, I have underlined the words that are identical in Jean Autret's French translation of Baldwin. Unlike the cases of Greene and MacDonald, I do not think there is hard evidence to show that Ouologuem borrowed from the existing French translation; the choices ("arme" for "weapon," "venin" for "venom," for example) could perhaps have been made by any translator. But the French translation existed at the time, and it seems more than likely that Ouologuem used it.

Bertrand writes of this case: "le plagiat ne reproduit pas, il transforme et réécrit." |

82 *Thresholds*

alors, ni le Dieu blanc
lui-même, ni une
foule accourue pour le
lyncher. A mi-voix, il
maudit cette chienne
d'un blanc de lait et
poussa un grognement
en faisant **aller son
arme entre les cuisses
de la femme.** Elle se mit
à pleurer. 'Je te l'avais
dit, gronda-t-il, que je
te ferais pleurer pour
quelque chose," et,
aussitôt, il sentit qu'il
manquait d'air; il allait
exploser ou mourir.
Un gémissement un
juron s'échappèrent
pendant qu'il la
martelait de toutes ses
forces, et sentit **le venin
jaillir,** assez de venin
pour faire cent bébés
nègres-blancs."

James Baldwin,
Another Country
(New York: Vintage
Books, 1960), 21-22.

**"And she carried him,
as the sea will carry
a boat: with a slow,
rocking and rising
and falling motion,
barely suggestive of the
violence of the deep.
They murmured and
sobbed on this journey,**
he softly, insistently
cursed. Each labored to
reach a harbor; there
could be no rest until
**this motion became
unbearably accelerated
by the power that was
rising in them both.**
Rufus opened his eyes
for a

A "Complete" Table   83

moment and watched her face, which was transfigured with agony and gleamed in the darkness like alabaster. Tears hung in the corners of her eyes and the hair at her brow was wet. Her breath came with moaning and short cries, with words he could not understand; and in spite of himself, he began **moving faster and thrusting deeper.** He wanted her to remember him the longest day she lived. And, shortly, nothing could have stopped him, not the white God himself nor lynch mob arriving on wings. Under his breath he cursed the milk-white bitch and **groaned and rode his weapon between her thighs.** She began to cry. 'I told you', he moaned, 'I'd give you something to cry about', and, at once, **he felt himself strangling, about to explode or die.** A moan and a curse tore through him while he beat her with all the strength he had and felt **the venom shoot out** of him, enough for a hundred black-white babies."

pp. 57–58
"Puis, l'après-midi, lorsque l'évêque Thomas de Saignac [...] la demeure qui lui avait été destine."

Habumukiza compares this to the Gospel According to Mark 11:7–11.

84 Thresholds

p. 59 "S'il est vrai, ergote-t-il d'une voix dialecticienne, s'il est vrai que le peuple de Cham [...] que nous puissions lutter contre l'homme blanc?"		Habumukiza compares this to the Old Testament, 2 *Chronicles*, 9: 1–12.
p. 67 "Dès qu'il la vit ..." Here begins a major section of plagiarism of Graham Greene. The first borrowed words are «et lui posa doucement la main sur le genou.» There are many adaptive paraphrases in Ouologuem's borrowings from Greene.	Graham Greene, *It's a Battlefield* (London: Heinemann, 1934), 57. "The kitchen was like a snowdrift [...] and half a loaf is better than no bread." As explained in the preface to this table, I am convinced that Ouologuem borrowed from the French translation of Greene: *C'est un champ de bataille*, by Marcelle Sibon (Paris: Robert Laffont, 1953).	See Habumukiza's thesis, Annexe 1, for a table of comparisons between (N.B.) the French translation of Greene's novel—*C'est un champ de bataille* (1957)—and DV. And see his chapter on this. Also see Bertrand, Annexe. See my analysis of this in *Blank Darkness*, 220–22. See also Seth Wolitz, "L'art du plagiat, ou une brève defense de Ouologuem," *Research in African Literatures* 4, no. 1 (Spring 1973): 132. Wolitz conducts a very close, line-by-line reading of the passage beginning "La cuisine évoquait" and ending "vers Saïf"—alongside the passage from *It's a Battlefield* (the English original, not the French translation) from which it was taken.
pp. 68 "J'habite ici tout seul, fit-il d'un air triste et un peu guindé, ma femme est morte. (Il craqua une allumette, introduisit la flamme dans une lampe à pétrole, et **des murs blancs montèrent autour d'eux**.) **Prenez** les oranges pendant que j'allume les autres lampes. (95) **Il s'agenouilla** auprès de quatre autres appareils, et **les douces flammes** crépitèrent **au bout de son allumette, avec un sifflement**. [...] C'est pas mal **chez vous**, susurra effrontément Awa. Ce que **vous en avez des livres!**	Greene trans., p. 88 "J'habite ici tout seul, fit-il d'un air triste et un peu guindé, ma femme est morte. Il tourna un commutateur et **des murs blancs montèrent autour d'eux**.) **Prenez** une noisette **pendant que j'allume** le feu. **Il s'agenouilla** et **les douces flammes** jaillirent du **bout de son allumette avec un sifflement**. "C'est très joli, **chez vous** , dit Kay Rimmer. Ce que **vous en avez des livres!**"	And for the public exposure of the plagiarism of Greene, see the anonymous "Something *New* Out of Africa?", *Times Literary Supplement*, May 5, 1972. The story was picked up by the *New York Times* the same day, quoting the publisher of the American edition, William Jovanovich, saying, "If I can not warrant it, I can not publish it." He "got rid" of the remaining 3,400 copies of *Bound to Violence*. Quoted in Thomas Mallon, *Stolen Words: Forays into the Origins and Ravages of Plagiarism* (New York: Ticknor & Fields, 1989), 123.

A "Complete" Table   85

—Ce sont tous ceux que j'ai écrits, mentit l'administrateur.
—Ce doit être merveilleux d'écrire.
—On tente de dire quelque chose. Euh … Aimeriez-vous visiter la maison? Elle est d'excellent goût, n'est-ce pas?
Naturellement, ajouta Chevalier baissant la voix, il y manque le cachet féminin.

The borrowing from Greene continues; I skip forward to this passage:

p. 69
"Oh! dit-elle, apercevant une glace aux reflets profonds, qui la flattait mieux que tout homme aux paroles doucereuses.
Aôôh! gloussa-t-elle, à la vue du seul tableau accroché au mur. Comme elle est jolie! Qui est-ce?
—Ma femme, répondit Chevalier, sans la regarder.
   Le portrait était juste face au lit. C'était le premier visage qui frappait au réveil. Ce visage lui disait bonjour le matin, lui faisait don de sa beauté, de sa malignité, de sa vertu."

—Ce sont ceux que j'ai écrits, expliqua Mr. Surrogate.
—Ce doit être merveilleux d'écrire.
—On tente d'exercer une influence. Aimeriez-vous visiter l'appartement? il est petit, mais de bon goût, je trouve. Naturellement, ajouta Mr. Surrogate baissant la voix respectueusement, il y manque le cachet féminin, c'est une tanière d'homme. (88)

p. 89
"Oh! fit-elle, apercevant le grand miroir aux reflets profonds qui la flattait plus qu'un homme aux paroles douces.
—Oh! fit-elle encore, à la vue du seul tableau accroché au mur. Comme elle est jolie! Qui est-ce?
—Ma femme, répondit Mr. Surrogate sans la regarder. Le portrait était juste en face du lit. C'était le premier visage qu'il voyait au réveil. Ce visage, avant Davis, lui disait bonjour le matin, en lui faisant le don de sa beauté, de sa malignité, de son intégrité."

Response by Ouologuem in *Le Figaro littéraire* (June 10, 1972). This is where he defends himself with the claim about quotation marks. (See Miller, *Blank Darkness*, section "The Purloined Quotation Marks," pp. 223–25.)

Roger Little writes: "I had the opportunity to ask Graham Greene about his reaction to being plagiarized by Ouologuem when we met at the Senate House in Paris in 1983 on the occasion of the award of the Prix Europa (for him) and the Bourse Europa (for me). It did not bother him in the least. Extending Keats's celebrated metaphor (in his letter of 27 February 1818 to John Taylor) of poetry coming as naturally as leaves to a tree, he suggested that those leaves became public property as they fell." Roger Little, "Reflections on a Triangular Trade in Borrowing and Stealing: Textual Exploitation in a Selection of African, Caribbean, and European Writers in French," *Research in African Literatures* 37, no. 1 (Spring 2006): 25 n. 11.

This reported conversation reflects an attitude on Greene's part that differs greatly from the position he was said to have taken in 1972. But Greene did not actually take legal action; he didn't have to: Seuil and the other publishers suppressed the novel on their own. When the scandal broke, Ouologuem bitterly complained to his editor at Seuil that they were proceeding to destroy his novel "sans la moindre réclamation de M. Graham Greene." Quoted in Orban, "Livre culte," para. 102.

86 Thresholds

"Comme vous avez dû l'aimer! hasarda Awa, fascinée par **ce visage. Et pendant un moment,** Chevalier **eut envie de** lui crier **la vérité: que** sa femme était là non parce qu'il l'adorait mais parce que le tableau ne pouvait être ailleurs, parce qu'il **lui rappelait l'unique** créature **qui avait lu clair en lui."**

pp. 89–90
"Comme vous avez dû l'aimer**, dit doucement Kay Rimmer sous le charme de **ce visage, et pendant un moment,** Mr. Surrogate **eut envie de lui** dire **la vérité: que** le tableau pendait là en expiation de la haine qu'il ressentait, et pour nourrir son humilité, parce qu'il **lui rappelait l'unique** femme **qui avait** *vu* **clair en lui."**

Since it was the "plagiarizing" of Greene that brought down *DV*, Tobias Warner's question is important: "Why did Ouologuem bother with this description [taken from Greene]?" Why did he go to the trouble to copy this anodyne passage? See "Bodies and Tongues: Alternative Modes of Translation in Francophone African Literature," in *Translation, Biopolitics, Colonial Difference*, ed. Naoki Sakai (Hong Kong: Hong Kong University Press, 2006), 308. Warner's answer to the question is: "The Graham Greene

---

p. 69
"Venez, que je vous montre **la cuisine,** se dépêcha-t-il d'éluder. **La cuisine** évoquait **un paysage de** rêve, **avec ses fenêtres blanches, son buffet blanc,** son ensemble blanc, son four à charbon **émaillé, ses murs et son plafond bleu** pastel.
   Par l'écartement des rideaux, **Awa aperçut,** dans la maison voisine, **qui se brossait les cheveux,** une splendide négresse nue, devant un miroir: un vaste **lit** à **deux personnes attendait ses** abonnés. Une ordonnance **mettait la table pour le** petit **déjeuner du** lendemain; ailleurs, le capitaine Vandame **écrivait,** devant un caporal au garde-à-vous.
   "Ils font tous quelque chose de différent,"** murmura-t-elle, cependant que son regard revenait au **grand lit, et ses pensées vers la courtepointe* rose, dans** la **chambre** de Chevalier, puis **vers** Saïf."

p. 90
"Venez, que je vous montre la cuisine,** dit-il vivement.

La cuisine ressemblait *à* **un paysage de** neige, **avec ses fenêtres blanches, son buffet blanc,** sa table blanche, son fourneau à gaz **émaillé, ses murs et son plafond** peints en bleu foncé. [...]
   Par l'écartement des rideaux** elle apercevait, à l'étage supérieur, une femme **qui se brossait les cheveux;** un grand **lit pour deux personnes attendait ses** occupants; une bonne **mettait la table pour le** déjeuner **du matin;** un homme écrivait des lettres; un chauffeur s'appuyait à la fenêtre d'un petit logement au-dessus d'un garage et fumait sa dernière pipe.
   "Ils font tous quelque chose de différent,"** dit-elle, tandis que ses yeux retournaient vers le **grand lit, et ses pensées vers la courte-pointe*** [Greene wrote: "bedspread"]

passages ignited the controversy and censorship because they were an incident of plagiarism-as-translation" (311). To Warner's excellent analysis I would add that, from the beginning of the scandal—the beginning being the exposé in the London *Times*—the missing link in Anglophone scholarship on this has been attention to the *French translations* from which Ouologuem evidently borrowed. It would be interesting to consider how it would affect Warner's theory if, in fact, Ouologuem had not (literally) *translated* Greene for himself but instead, as I believe, relied on the existing French translation.

Joel Bertrand (in 1984) also assumed that Ouologuem produced his own translation of Greene. See Bertrand's analysis of the "intertextuality" between Greene and Ouologuem: "L'intertextualité dans *Le Devoir de violence*," https://joelbertrand.wordpress.com/lintertextualite-dans-le-devoir-de-violence/.

If there is one "tell" in this passage, indicating that Ouologuem was working with the existing French translation, it is the choice of the French word *courtepointe* for Greene's "bedspread." The latter is a very generic term in English; there are dozens of types of bedspreads, of which a quilted *courtepoint* is but one. Along with dozens of

After introducing a passage and a scene borrowed from Robbe-Grillet's *La Maison de rendez-vous* (see below), Ouologuem returns with more words from Greene:	rose dans l'autre chambre et vers Jules, mais un demi-pain vaut mieux que pas du tout de pain, et que la ravissante et indifférente femme morte, dans son cadre.	other choices, this makes it seem unlikely that both Marcelle Sibon and Yambo Ouologuem would have produced the same rendering. I therefore believe that Ouologuem had the French translation of Greene's novel in front of him as he was writing *Le Devoir de violence*.
p. 71 "**La paix profonde de la volupté noya toutes les craintes, toutes les perplexités de la journée**; et la femme avoua **ne se sentir jamais aussi bien à sa place que dans** un **lit et dans les bras d'un homme.**"	Le corps de Kay était prêt pour le plaisir; **la paix profonde de la volupté noie toutes les craintes, toutes les perplexités de la** journée écoulée; Kay **ne se sentait jamais aussi bien à sa place que dans le lit et dans les bras d'un homme.**"	Another question about translation: does the Manheim translation of *Le Devoir de violence* take us "back" to Greene's original English? Of course not. For example: Greene: "The kitchen was like a snowdrift with its white casement and white dresser and white table and enamelled gas stove and its deep blue walls and ceiling" (p. 57); Manheim (after Ouologuem): "With its white windows, its white cupboards and tables, its enameled coal stove, and its pastel blue walls and ceiling, the kitchen seemed to emerge from a dream" (p. 55).
The sex scene involving dogs: p. 70 "Caressant la coupe creuse du ventre de la femme, il [Chevalier] baisa les longues ailes noires de sa nuque et sortit—revint avec deux setters, **chiens** beaux et robustes, et une camisole. Les bêtes dardaient sur eux leurs prunelles avides. Leur maître siffla et Médor s'élança sur Awa, gueule humide et frémissante. "Médor! jappa-t-il, vas-y! Quartier libre!"	Alain Robbe-Grillet, *La Maison de rendez-vous* (Paris: Editions de Minuit, 1965), 42–43. "Le **chien** s'est aussitôt dressé sur ses pattes en grondant. Deux jeunes femmes apparaissent à ce moment derrière la grille, que l'une d'elles—la plus grande—ouvre afin de leur livrer passage à toutes les deux tandis qu'elle pousse sa compagne en avant; la porte est ensuite refermée avec des bruite métalliques de gonds grinçants, de battant qui claque et de cadenas. Bientôt on ne	Habumukiza, 88; Bertrand, Annexe 4.XIII. Here the borrowing is mostly thematic, with little textual reproduction. This could well be called a pastiche of Robbe-Grillet. Further, the influence of *La Maison de rendez-vous* on Ouologuem's *Mille et une bibles du sexe* is obvious. For analysis of this passage in *DV*, see Robert Philipson, "Chess and Sex in *Le Devoir du* [sic] *violence*," *Callaloo* 39 (Winter 1989): 216–32.

88 *Thresholds*

Avant que la femme pût réaliser quoi que ce fût, elle sentit le mufle du setter et **ses crocs** mettre en pièce ses **vêtements**, déchirant son pagne et sa camisole, la dénudant à coup de griffes et de pattes, sans érafler la peau. Il devait avoir une habitude peu commune de ce genre de travail, Médor.

distingue plus personne, les deux filles ayant été absorbées par l'ombre l'une après l'autre, à partir des jambes, sitôt qu'elles ont commence à descendre l'escalier; elles ne reparaissent que tout en bas de celui-ci, dans la clarté des projecteurs: ce sont bien entendu la servante eurasienne et la petite Japonaise. La première détache sans attendre le bout de la tresse de cuir [...] pendant que la nouvelle arrivante, effrayée par les grondements menaçants de l'animal, se réfugie contre le mûr du fond [...] où elle se plaque dos à la pierre. Le **chien**, qui a pour cela subi *un dressage spécial*, doit *déshabiller* entièrement la prisonnière, que lui désigne la servante de son bras libre, pointé vers la jupe à plis; jusqu'au dernier triangle de soie, il déchire avec **ses crocs** les **vêtements** et les arrache par lambeaux, peu à peu, sans blesser les chairs.

	Guy de Maupassant, "Le Rosier de Mme Husson," *Contes et nouvelles*, 2:961–62.	Bertrand, Annexe 4.I.
p. 75 (1968)		
"Le repas continua, interminable, magnifique, véritable **banquet. Les plats suivaient les plats;** le champagne et le **vin** blanc **fraternisaient dans les verres voisins et se mêlaient dans les estomacs** des invités. [...] **Le choc d'assiettes, les voix, et la musique qui jouait en sourdine, faisaient une rumeur continue, profonde, s'éparpillant dans le ciel clair**—où **volèrent** les notes du clairon, sonnant le couvre-feu. **Mme** Vandame **rajustait**, fascinée par Saïf, son corsage où dansaient ses seins, et le commandant, **excité, parlait politique** cependant que Saïf **mangeait** mais ne buvait point. **Il prenait et reprenait de tout**, grattant la surface des plats, comme s'il venait de **s'apercevoir** qu'il était habile de feindre l'ignorance, de croire si **doux de sentir son ventre s'emplir de bonnes choses, qui font plaisir d'abord en passant par la bouche.**	"Il [le **banquet**] fut **interminable et magnifique. Les plats suivaient les plats;** le cidre jaune et le **vin** rouge **fraternisaient dans les verres voisins et se mêlaient dans les estomacs. Les chocs d'assiettes, les voix et la musique qui jouait en sourdine faisaient une rumeur continue, profonde, s'éparpillant dans le ciel clair où** volaient les hirondelles. **Mme** Husson **rajustait** par moments sa perruque de soie noire chavirée sur une oreille et causait avec l'abbé Malou. Le maire, **excité, parlait politique** avec le commandant Desbarres, et Isidore **mangeait**, Isidore buvait, comme il n'avait jamais bu et mangé! **Il prenait et reprenait de tout**, s'apercevant pour la première fois qu'il est **doux de sentir son ventre s'emplir de bonnes choses qui font plaisir d'abord en** passant dans **la bouche.**	
[Minor borrowings continue on p. 75.]		
p. 80 "il n'y a ni Juif ni Noir"	New Testament: Galatians (St. Paul's letter to) 3:28: "In Christ there is nor Jew nor Greek." Paul is quoted on p. 81.	On Ouologuem's borrowings from and allusions to the Bible, see Habumukiza, ch. 4, and Bertrand, Annexe 4.XV.

90 Thresholds

p. 80 "Il y eut une pluie et il y eut une sécheresse: deuxième an [...] un seul chef—aidé de tous."	Gospel According to John 1:8, 9, 12, 14. "He [John the Baptist] was not that Light, but was sent witness to that Light, which lighteth every man that cometh into the world. He was in the world ... But as many as received him, to them have him power to become sons of God ... And the word was made flesh, and dwelt among us."	This comparison is made by Chaulet-Achour, 103. See also Habumukiza, 70. But it seems to me that the first sentence quoted here ("Il y eut sécheresse ... deuxième an") is more obviously an allusion to Genesis 1, the creation story (the first day, the second day, etc.).
p. 81 "Saïf dit: "Que les mission-naires [...] troisième an."	Genesis 1:11–13. "Ainsi, il y eut un soir, et il y eut un matin : ce fut le troisième jour."	Habumuzika, 71.
p. 95 "Il la fit asseoir, et lui **posa** doucement **la main sur le genou**. La lampe à pression, amenée par un soldat, **coupa d'une barre de lumière l'intérieur sombre de** l'antichambre; et Chevalier **apercevant le sourire d'attente de sa compagne, retira vivement sa main. Pas de gestes inconsidérés: il est si facile de faire naître un malentendu**, à pas feutrés, **il la précéda** dans la véranda **qui menait au** salon et autres pièces de la maison."	Greene, *It's a Battlefield*, Sibon translation, p. 87 "il [Mr Surrogate] **posa** amicalement **la main sur le genou** de Kay Rimmer. Un réverbère **coupa d'une barre de lumière l'intérieur sombre** de la voiture et Mr. Surrogate, **apercevant le sourire d'attente de sa compagne, retira vivement sa main. Pas de gestes inconsidérés: il est si facile de faire naître un malentendu**; et **il la précéda** à pas très doux, **dans** l'escalier **qui menait au** premier étage de l'immeuble divisé en appartements." Ouologuem continues to borrow from subsequent pages of this section of *It's a Battlefield*, 88–90, in DV, 68–69. See above.	Habumuzika, 84–85. Adaptive paraphrases are to be noted in this passage (*amicalement* becomes *doucement* ; *à pas très doux* becomes *à pas feutrés*, etc.).

A "Complete" Table 91

p. 104	Guy de Maupassant, "Marroca," in *Contes et nouvelles*, 1:367. Second use of this story in *DV*.	See Bertrand, Annexe 4.III.
"Ils ne se disaient rien et restaient l'un en face de l'autre, la tête baissée, le regard indécis, comme perdus en une difficile méditation, sentant du nouveau dans l'air, respirait de l'invisible,— avertissement mystérieux qui les prévint de leurs intentions secrètes, les paralysait dans **une sorte d'ardeur frémissante**, de **soulèvement**—en cette **brusque tension** qui **court au bout des doigts, surexcité à les exaspérer toutes** les **facultés de sensation physique, jusqu'à cet innommable besoin** de **commettre des sottises**."	"Tu m'as écrit, dans ta dernière lettre: 'Quand je sais comment on aime dans un pays, je connais ce pays à le décrire, bien que ne l'ayant jamais vu.' Sache qu'ici on aime furieusement. On sent, dès les premiers jours, **une sorte d'ardeur frémissante, un soulèvement, une brusque tension** des désirs, un énervement **courant au bout des doigts, qui surexcitent à les exaspérer** nos puissances amoureuses et **toutes nos facultés de sensation physique,** depuis le simple contact des mains **jusqu'à cet innommable besoin qui nous fait commettre** tant de **sottises**."	
pp. 100ff. "Fritz Schrobénius"	The German Africanist Leo Frobenius, who was so influential on Léopold Sédar Senghor and on Aimé and Suzanne Césaire. A textual borrowing appears below, p. 111. Here the paraphrase is exact: "Il considérait que la vie africaine était art pur" (102). Frobenius wrote about the Kasai region of Congo in 1906: "each cup, each pipe, each spoon is a work of art." ("Die Kunst Afrikas," *Der Erdball* 3 (1931): 90).	See my analysis of Frobenius/ Schrobénius in *Theories of Africans*, 16–21. See also Elizabeth Harney, *In Senghor's Shadow: Art, Politics, and the Avant-Garde in Senegal, 1960–1995* (Durham, NC: Duke University Press, 2004), 30.

The scathing portrait of Schrobénius was no doubt provoked by this quality of Frobenius: "Hostile à tout changement, à toute modernisation, Frobenius veille directement sur les anciennes traditions [africaines] et s'établit le 'protecteur' de ses découvertes." (Hans-Jürgen Heinrichs, *Leo Frobenius: Anthropologue, explorateur, aventurier,* trans. Catherine and Marie-Pierre Emery (Paris: L'Harmattan, 1999), 70–71)

Ouologuem would not have had to read Frobenius directly: in the first issue of the wartime journal edited by Aimé and Suzanne Césaire, *Tropiques* (April 1941) Suzanne devoted an article to "Léo Frobenius et le problème des civilisations."

The views attributed to Schrobénius sound not only like those of Frobenius, but also like those of Placide Tempels, the Belgian priest who wrote *La Philosophie bantoue.* Given the timing and the controversies surrounding the latter work, it would be surprising if Ouologuem did not make use of it. But I do not know of specific passages in *DV* that were inspired by Tempels.

Graham Huggan suggests that Ouologuem had two other German anthropologists in mind, as well as Frobenius: "*Fritz* Graebner and Father Wilhelm *Sch*midt [...] These three men are lampooned by Ouologuem in the composite figure of Fritz Schrobénius." See "Anthropologists and Other Frauds, *Comparative Literature* 46, no. 2 (1994): 117.

Kyle Wanberg calls this a "devastating critique of the xenophilic cult of authenticity and its expertise in Africanism"; *Maps of Empire: A Topography of World Literature* (Toronto: University of Toronto Press, 2020), 73.

A *"Complete" Table*   93

p. 106	Violette Leduc, *Thérèse et Isabelle* (Paris: Gallimard, 1966).	Bertrand, Annexe 4.XIV. Here Bertrand truly found a needle in a haystack.
"Tiens mes doudounes, tu les aimes, **mon petit mongoli**. Continue ... là ... oui, là, goûte à sa chair réelle, fais moi **vomir les délices de son orgasme**. Ça te plaît, dis. Tu veux bien, n'est-ce pas?"	pp. 50, 51–52 "Tu sens ma joue sur toi, **mon petit mongoli?** Je te peigne, je te démêle, je te cajole, mon petit mordoré ... Tu brilles, Isabelle, tu brilles [...] Bientôt **je vomirais les délices de son orgasme**."	This short, pornographic novel by Leduc has its own strange history: it was originally part of a longer work, *Ravages*, which was censored by Gallimard (by the writer and editor Raymond Queneau). *Ravages* was published in 1955 without its opening parts, which were later published as *Thérèse et Isabelle*. A restored, complete edition of *Ravages* was published by Gallimard in 2023.
p. 106	A. Waltraut, *La Bavaroise* (Paris: La Sirène, 1961), 16–17.	Bertrand, Annexe 4.XIV bis. See above, *Thérèse et Isabelle*; this is a very similar case of amazing sleuthing by Bertrand.
"'[...] Viens, happe de tes bonnes lèvres gourmandes **l'arc tendu de leur bosquet blond parfumé et touffu**, où tu **dors, mon trésor. Encore!** haletait-il se cabrant dans les airs. **Oh! encore, je t'en supplie, embrasse là!** Bécote, lèche, foudre qui foudroie mes entrailles et révèle l'auréole de mon ventre. **Tiens mes doudounes**, tu les aimes, mon petit mongoli. Continue ... là ... oui, là, goûte à sa chair réelle, fais moi vomir les délices de son orgasme. Ça te plaît, dis. Tu veux bien, n'est-ce pas?' Et il ronronnait sous ses propres caresses, se lovant en tous sens, frottant ses jambes l'une contre l'autre— et **toute sa chair vibrait comme la corde d'une harpe adroitement pincée**, *joliment* **caressée**."	"Puis, lorsqu'**elle relâchait mes doudounes**, je faisais le pont de mon jeune corps et dressais sous son visage empourpré **l'arc tendu de** ma frise boisée où, **sous un bosquet blond, parfumé et touffu, dormait mon trésor**. Ce jour-là, pour la première fois, Nounou se pencha sur ma corolle et posa sa bouche sur ma féminité. [...] —**Encore! haletai-je** lorsqu'elle voulut se retirer. **Oh encore, je t'en supplie** Nounou, c'est si bon, et caresse-moi pendant que tu m'**embrasses là!** Oh! Oh! Encore, je t'en supplie, n'arrête jamais plus, je veux mourir ainsi sous ta bouche! **Toute ma chair vibrait comme la corde d'une harpe adroitement pincée**, *aimablement* **caressée**."	This (no doubt pseudonymous) author is unknown. The novel is lesbian-erotic with an aristocratic context, much as in Ouologuem's later *Les mille et une bibles du sexe*. (As Joël Bertrand pointed out to me, the name "A. Waltraut" suggests "avale trop.")

94 Thresholds

p. 111

Leo Frobenius, *Histoire de la civilization africaine*, trans. H. Back and E. Ermont (Paris: Gallimard, 1936), 14:

Joseph R. Slaughter, "'It's Good to Be Primitive': African Allusion and the Modernist Fetish of Authenticity," in *Modernism & Copyright*, ed. Paul K. Saint-Amour (Oxford: Oxford University Press, 2011), 293.

"Mais l'audience du Tout-Puissant est infinie, qui comblant les vœux de tout ce monde, souffla a Shrobénius l'intuition lunatiquement géniale de clamer, parlant du Nakem, de sa civilisation et de son passé: 'Mais ces gens sont policés, **civilisés jusqu'aux os!** Partout, avenues larges, calmes, paisibles, ou l'on respire la grandeur d'un peuple, son génie humain [...].'"

"Plus au Sud, dans le Royaume du Congo, une foule grouillante habillée de 'soie' et de 'velours,' de grands Etats bien ordonnés, et cela dans les moindres détails, des souverains puissants, des industries opulentes. **Civilisés jusqu'à** la moelle des **os!**"

This phrase was quoted by Aimé Césaire in his *Discours sur le colonialism* (Paris: Présence Africaine, 1955 [1950]), 30, and by Léopold Sédar Senghor in "Les Leçons de Léo Frobénius," *Présence Africaine* 111 (1979): 146.

Frobenius was immensely influential with the founders of Negritude, including Aimé and Suzanne Césaire and Senghor. Suzanne published "Léo Frobenius et le problème des civilisations" in the first issue of *Tropiques* (April 1941): 27–36. And a translation of Frobenius, "Que signifie pour nous l'Afrique?", taken from *Histoire de la civilization africaine*, appeared in *Tropiques* 5 (April 1942): 62–70.

---

p. 123
"Le Sud. Le Sud."

This is a theme in *Le Regard du roi*, the novel attributed to, but probably not written by Camara Laye (Paris: Presses Pocket, 1954), 243. (See my book *Impostors*). The association of the South with salvation is shared by both texts. Also shared: the notion of the *juste*, found in *DV* many, many times including p. 133, and *Regard*, p. 248. The embrace of the king at the end of *Le Regard* is also reminiscent of the embrace of the leper,

A "Complete" Table   95

	who turns out to be Christ, at the end of Flaubert's *La Légende de Saint-Julien l'Hospitalier*, 130-31.	
p. 128	Raymond Chandler, *Le Grand sommeil*, trans. Boris Vian (Paris: Gallimard, 1948), 44.	Bertrand, Annexe 4.XI.
"Vandame se frotta la nuque et grimaça. Il **portait des pantoufles chinoises à épaisses semelles de feutre; ses jambes emplissaient un pyjama de satin noir, et** son buste était revêtu d'une **tunique chinoise brodée—au plastron** blanc."	"Geiger **portait des pantoufles chinoises à épaisses semelles de feutre; ses jambes emplissaient un pyjama de satin noir** et la partie supérieure de son individu était revêtue d'une **tunique chinoise brodée, au plastron** presque entièrement couvert de sang."	
p. 130	John MacDonald, *Les Energumènes*, trans. Janine Hérisson (Paris: Gallimard, Série Noire, 1962). The original is *The End of the Night* (Greenwich, CT: Fawcett Publications, 1960), 129–35. p. 166	My thanks to Jean-Pierre Orban, whose notes taken from the Ouologuem papers at IMEC, which he kindly shared, allowed me to find this obscure passage. Bertrand had already identified the passage, in fact. See his Annexe 4.XII. Letter from Claude Gallimard to Paul Flamand, quoted and reproduced in Orban, para. 116. Ouologuem claims that the name of John MacDonald appeared in the 1963 ms that was rejected by Seuil. See Orban, reprint of Ouologuem letter, para. 132. It is not clear what bearing that would have had on any accusation of plagiarism.
"—Voilà une attitude **mesquine, mon** petit. Comment? Tu joues les moralistes quand **tu as justement l'occasion** de t'amuser un peu? —M'amuser? —**Nous sommes tes nouveaux amis**, mec. **Traite tes amis comme il faut,** Vandame. —**D'accord, fit-il, ayant l'air de prendre sa mésaventure avec philosophie. Ça peut être** une causerie amicale, **si vous voulez.**"	"—Voilà une attitude **mesquine, mon** vieux. Tu es un homme d'affaires et un clubman prospère. Et **tu as justement l'occasion** de nous prêter une voiture et un peu d'argent. —Prêter? —**Nous sommes tes nouveaux amis. Traite tes amis comme il faut,** Tex. —**D'accord,** dit-il en **ayant l'air de prendre sa mésaventure avec philosophie. Ça peut être** un prêt, **si vous voulez.**	In MacDonald's novel, a band of desperados is on a murderous cross-country crime spree when they accost Horace Beecher, a "traveling salesman, a bowler, and a family man." (Eerily, this takes place near Uvalde, Texas, the site of yet another American mass school shooting, in 2021.) They seemingly murder him for the thrill of it.

96   *Thresholds*

Depuis un moment, il se rapprochait insensiblement du pistolet. Kratonga l'avait remarqué, et Wampoulo aussi, sans doute. Soudain il pivota et plongea tête la première sur le roc pour se saisir de l'arme. Il la prit, la braqua sur les deux hommes, appuya sur la gachette, tira, appuya encore, tira, trois fois de suite. Puis ses mains ralentirent leurs mouvements et s'immobilisèrent. Il demeura un instant à moitié couché sur le roc, comme épuisé. On l'entendit haleter. Puis il se redressa lentement, avec une espèce de sombre désespoir, et adressa aux deux hommes un sourire bien pénible à voir. "Voilà qui était fort discourtois, gouverneur," opina Kratonga, ramassant le pistolet, où il glissa le chargeur, qu'il exhiba à Vandame ahuri.

Une hyène, très loin dans la brousse, fit entendre une plainte assourdie. Vandame demeurait planté dans la plaque d'ombre de son propre corps. Il transpirait abondamment. La situation était en train d'évoluer. C'était lui qui avait déclenché la brusque accélération.

Kratonga se dirigea vers l'un des chevaux, tirant de son harnais une grosse flute de bambou et une outre. Le gouverneur se retourna, le vit et lui intima, avec une autorité toute machinale: 'Finissons-en, voulez-vous.' [...]

Depuis un moment, il se rapprochait insensiblement de la portière ouverte de la voiture. Je l'avais remarqué, et Sandy aussi, sans doute. Soudain, il pivota et plongea la tête la première sur la banquette pour ouvrir la boîte à gants. Il se mit à y fouiller des deux mains; il fit jaillir une pluie de prospectus, déplaça une boîte de Kleenex, un flacon d'huile solaire, des cartes routières.

Puis ses mains ralentirent leurs mouvements et s'immobilisèrent. Il demeura un instant à moitié couché sur la banquette, comme épuisé. On l'entendit haleter. Puis il se redressa lentement pour s'extraire de la voiture et nous adressa un petit sourire bien pénible à voir.

—Voilà qui n'était guère poli, mec, dit Sandy.

The substitutions—of a hyena for a jet airplane, and of a viper for a can of shaving cream—are to be noted with amusement. I see these as evidence of a strategy of stealthy, satiric response to Seuil's demand: be more African. It is almost as if Ouologuem were saying, "Here, take a hyena; is that 'African' enough for you?"

This is the passage to which translator Ralph Manheim added numerous lines of his own invention, including a borrowing from Emily Dickinson; see my essay.

'Je peux vous le marquer par écrit. La libération de Sankolo et les témoignages de ma femme. Nous n'avons rien vu, nous ne savons rien. Comme ça vous aurez une prévue […].'"	p. 167 Un avion à réaction, très haut dans le ciel, faisait entendre une sorte de déchirement assourdi. Beecher demeurait planté dans la plaque d'ombre de son corps. Il transpirait abondamment. La situation était en train d'évoluer. C'était lui qui avait déclenché ce changement. Mon estomac se noua et se révulsa.
p. 131 "Tu n'es pas en forme, observa Katonga [sic]. Tu as besoin de te remonter, pas vrai? Bois un peu, rien qu'une goutte. —Je ne crois pas que … —Tu vas avoir des ennuis, Vandame. Allons, bois." Kratonga se rapprochait de lui. Vandame souleva donc l'outre… Baissant les yeux, il vit, horrifié, une vipère aspic. Il s'immobilisa, cramoisi, devant le reptile […]."	Robert se dirigea vers le panneau arrière, le rabattit et en sortit une lourde boîte en carton. Horace se retourna, le vit et lui intima, avec une autorité toute machinale: —Faites attention à ça. […]
p. 132 "—Fais ça tous les jours et tu vivras plus vieux, déclara Kratonga. Tu feras ça tous les jours? —Oui, Monsieur, fit Vandame. Toute résistance l'avait abandonné. Il avait accepté l'humiliation; il ne lui restait plus grand-chose, hormis un désir aveugle d'être agréable à ses bourreaux et de tenir le coup […] —Je peux vous faire une attestation, reprit Vandame."	—Je peux vous le marquer par écrit. Le prêt de la voiture et de l'argent. Comme ça, vous aurez une prévue. […] p. 168 "—Tu n'es pas en forme, dit Sandy. Tu as besoin d'exercice. Quelqu'un a une idée?"

98   *Thresholds*

Cette phrase était une sorte de talisman, et il la psalmodiait **comme une prière, sans grand espoir.**

—Je peux vous mettre tout ça par écrit."

Brusquement Kratonga saisit Dafa [the viper] et la lança sur Vandame. La vipère **lui rebondit contre la poitrine avant de tomber à terre,** d'où elle enlaça le gouverneur.

"Défais le nœud, Vandame. Parfait. **Je t'adore,** Vandame. Tu es le juste du colonialisme.*

Ecarte-toi de cet honnête Wampoulo. Plus loin. Bravo, mon chou. T'es épatant, mec. Nous allons jouer à Guillaume Tell. Il est une heure du matin. Allons enfants de la patrie. C'est le 14 juillet, gouverneur. Prends ton rapport sur Sa Seigneurie royale. Plus vite que ça. Chouette. Fais-en une

boule, Vandame. **Pose**-la **sur ta tête,** commandant."

Les yeux de Vandame semblèrent **lui jaillir de la tête:**

—Vous ne pouvez pas …
—Du calme, du calme, excité! **Je tire comme un chef,** mec.

Allez, **sur la tête! Je t'adore,** Vandame. Humaniste, gouverneur, ami de la libération des Noirs, civili-sateur du Nakem, marié et républicain!"

Vandame **restait les yeux fermés, bras ballants.** Son corps se dérobait sous lui. Contre son genou, Dafa.

p. 169
"**—Tu vas avoir des ennuis,** Horace. Allez! Va!

Robert **se rapprochait de lui.** Horace se décida donc. Il choisit un endroit mou pour poser la tête […] **Il s'arrêta, cramoisi,** tremblant, à bout de souffle
[…]

—Fais ça tous les jours et tu vivras plus vieux, déclara Sandy. **Tu feras ça tous les jours?**
—Oui, monsieur, dit Horace.

Toute résistance l'avait abandonné. Il avait accepté l'humiliation et il ne lui restait plus grand-chose, à part **un désir aveugle de** nous **être agréable.** Il espérait **tenir le coup,** et c'était tout […]

—Je peux vous faire un papier, pour la voiture, **reprit** Horace.

Cette phrase était une sorte de talisman, et il la répétait **comme une prière, sans grand espoir.**

—Je peux vous mettre tout ça par écrit.

* It is to be remembered that the most important and obvious borrowing in *Le Devoir de violence* comes from André Schwarz-Bart's *Le Dernier des Justes*. The concept of the *juste* or "righteous one" is repeated here by Ouologuem, perhaps with a wink. The word *juste* (in this sense) is used repeatedly in the early pages of Ouologuem's novel, then reappears here with reference to Vandame. The oxymoron of a "juste du coloni-alisme" (here juxtaposed to Horace Beecher's status as "the keystone of the modern South") invites reflection.

Kratonga fit crisser ses dents. **Le canon de l'automatique** décrivit **des cercles minuscules.** Kratonga **le tenait à bout de bras et visait avec** minutie.

Le pistolet émit un claquement **sec,** étouffé par le grondement de la cataracte. Vandame tressauta tel un forcené, et le rapport s'embrasa. Wampoulo l'éteignit, puis le lui fit **remettre** sur la tête. Kratonga **visa de nouveau.** Le pistolet aboya. **Un petit trou, rond apparut sur le front** du gouverneur, près du sourcil droit, à la naissance de la racine nasale. **Ses yeux** s'ent**rouvrirent,** le rapport glissa à terre, **il fit un pas** pour se relever, comme s'il voulait tenter de s'enfuir. **Puis il** s'affala doucement, et, un **instant** raide, tournoya sur lui-même, bavant contre le sable et tombant à la renverse, sur le ventre. Ses pieds raclèrent le roc, on entendit des borborygmes sortir du fond de sa gorge, **puis ses poumons se vidèrent en un long râle saccadé.** C'était un juste."

Sandy attrapa la bombe à raser et la lança sur Horace. Elle **lui rebondit contre la poitrine avant de tomber à terre.**

Ramasse, Horace. Parfait. **Je t'adore,** Horace. Tu es la clé de voûte du Sud moderne. **Ecarte-toi** de cette voiture. **Plus loin. Bravo, mon petit. Tu es épatant, mec. Nous allons jouer à Guillaume Tell.** Ecoutez le roulement des tambours, citoyens. **Pose** la bombe **sur la tête,** Horace!

Les yeux d'Horace semblaient **lui jaillir de la tête.**
—Vous ne pouvez **pas** ...
—Fais-moi confiance, mec. **Je tire comme un chef.** Allez, **sur la tête! Je t'adore.** Horace Beecher, commis voyageur, bouliste, père de famille.

Beecher **restait les yeux fermés,** les **bras ballants.** Il vacillait lentement. Sandy se mordit la lèvre. Je vis **le canon de l'automatique** décrire **des cercles minuscules.** Il le tenait **à bout de bras et visait avec soin.**

Le pistolet fit un bruit **sec,** à peine plus impressionnant que celui d'un jouet d'enfant. Horace sursauta violemment et la bombe tomba à terre. Sandy la lui fit ramasser et **remettre**

100 *Thresholds*

en place. Il **visa de nouveau.** Le pistolet fit de nouveau entendre son petit aboiement. **Un petit trou rond apparut sur le front** de Beecher, tout en haut, légèrement sur la gauche. **Ses yeux s'ouvrirent** au moment où la bombe tombait. Il fit un pas pour écarter les pieds, comme s'il voulait essayer de se mettre bien d'aplomb sur ses jambes.

Puis il s'effondra lentement, comme s'il tentait d'amortir sa chute. Il resta un **instant** appuyé sur un coude et se retourna sur le dos. Sa poitrine se souleva **puis ses poumons se vidèrent en long râle saccadé.**

---

pp. 140–41	Flaubert, "La Légende de Saint Julien l'Hospitalier," 121-22.	Habumukiza (79) calls this a mix of plagiarism and paraphrase. Of the last example he writes: "la transposition thématique est subordonnée au plagiat" (78).
"Il tendait la main aux soldats **sur** les pistes, ou, restant **immobile devant** le clos des champs, il se louait; **et son visage était si** las, et son corps bossu si frappant, **que jamais aumône** ne lui fut refusé.	**"Il tendait sa main aux** cavaliers **sur** les routes, avec des génuflexions s'approchait des moissonneurs, ou restait **immobile devant** la barrière des cours; et son visage était si triste **que jamais** on ne lui refusait l'**aumône.**	
Un soir à la veillée du village de Toula, il dit par **humilité** avoir laissé mourir Sankolo, avoir tué Barou venu se confesser à lui; alors tous le prirent pour fou et s'enfuirent, jurant par Saïf. Dans les hameaux où il	Par esprit **d'humilité,** il racontait son histoire; alors tous s'enfuyaient, en faisant des signes de croix. Dans les villages où il avait déjà	

A "Complete" Table   101

avait déjà passé, sitôt qu'il était reconnu, les enfants couraient à leurs mères, lesquelles, claquant les portes des cases, lui criaillaient des infamies. Les moins hargneux posaient une écuelle de mil au seuil de leur demeure, **puis** tiraient le loquet pour s'isoler de lui.

passé, sitôt qu'il était reconnu, on fermait **les portes**, on lui criait des menaces, on lui jetait des pierres. Les plus charitables **posaient une écuelle** sur le bord de leur fenêtre, puis fermaient l'auvent pour ne pas l'apercevoir.

Repoussé de partout, il continuait à donner des médicaments, dont nul indigène ne voulait plus désormais, venus de sa main; alors Henry **se nourrit** d'ignames, de patates, de fruits perdus, de racines diverses, restes laisses par les troupes en guerre. De loin en loin, il descendait dans les villages."

Repoussé de partout, il évita les hommes; et **il se nourrit** de racines, de plantes, de fruits perdus, et de coquillages qu'il cherchait le long des grèves.

pp. 141–42

"Henry **se fit un cilice avec des pointes de fer. Il** rampa **sur les deux genoux** dans chaque maison qui comptait plus de quatre greniers: maison de notable polygame. Il y obtint vivres et habits, vêtit les loqueteux et nourrit les affamés.

Il **se fit un cilice avec des pointes de fer. Il** monta **sur les deux genoux** toutes les collines ayant une chapelle à leur sommet. Mais l'impitoyable pensée obscurcissait la splendeur des tabernacles, le torturait à travers les macérations de la pénitence [...] (123).

Son visage était si ravagé, d'un aspect si lamentable que les siens ne pouvaient retenir leur pitié. Ils priaient et pleuraient, avançant pieusement parmi la terreur que semait la guerre."

Il tendait sa main aux cavaliers sur les routes, avec des génuflexions s'approchait des moissonneurs, ou restait immobile devant la barrière des cours; et **son visage était si** triste que jamais on ne lui refusait l'aumône." (121).

102 *Thresholds*

p. 144	Guy de Maupassant, "Boule de suif," *Contes et nouvelles* 1:86.	This case of intertextuality was one of the first to be identified. Original scholarship on this came from Christine Chaulet-Achour's dissertation: "Langue française et colonialisme en Algérie: de l'abécédaire à la production littéraire" (Université de Paris III, 1982), 2:419–43. I said in *Blank Darkness* (224 n.) that hers was "the most complete analysis of the intertextuality of *DV*." (Now superseded by Habumukiza and Bertrand.) Chaulet-Achour's essay cited above ("Writing as ..." in the Wise book) is "entirely reworked from a portion" of the thesis (as noted therein 106 n. 2).
"Parmi les décombres de la guerre, Kassoumi rêvassait sous son bananier, promenant, au-delà des feuillettes grisâtres des fruits bourgeonnants, son pauvre regard sur la rive du Yamé, empestée par l'odeur saumâtre de carcasses de squelettes que les **pêcheurs ramenaient souvent du fond de l'eau,** dans leurs filets, **cadavre d'Allemand** décomposé **dans son uniforme, tué d'un coup de** lance ou de sabre, **la tête écrasée par une pierre, ou** flanqué à l'eau **du haut d'un pont. Les vases du fleuve ensevelissaient ces vengeances obscures, sauvages héroïsmes inconnus,** attaques muettes, **plus périlleuses que les batailles au grand jour, et sans le retentissement de la gloire.**"	"Cependant, à deux ou trois lieues sous la ville, en suivant le cours de la rivière, vers Croisset, Dieppedalle ou Biessart, les mariniers et les **pêcheurs ramenaient souvent du fond de l'eau** quelque **cadavre d'Allemand** gonflé **dans son uniforme, tué d'un coup de** couteau ou de savate, **la tête écrasée par une pierre,** ou jeté à l'eau d'une poussée **du haut d'un pont. Les vases du fleuve ensevelissaient ces vengeances obscures, sauvages et légitimes, héroïsmes inconnus, attaques muettes, plus périlleuses que les batailles au grand jour et sans le retentissement de la gloire.**"	Habumukiza (98) discusses this Maupassant passage.
p. 144 (second paragraph)	Guy de Maupassant, "Le Champ d'oliviers," *Contes et nouvelles*, 2:1183–84.	Bertrand, Annexe 4.VI.
"**Ses idées pieuses** d'antan, **ardeur** apaisée de **sa foi première,** revinrent au cœur de Kassoumi, tout doucement. L'**instruction, qui lui était apparue comme un refuge contre** le servage, lui apparaissait à présent comme **un noble gagne-pain** dont vivraient ses enfants à l'abri de l'existence inconnue, **trompeuse et torturante** qu'avait été la sienne."	"Mais ses anciennes **idées pieuses, l'ardeur** un peu calmée de **sa foi première lui** revinrent au cœur tout doucement dans cette solitude douloureuse. **La religion qui lui était apparue** autrefois **comme un refuge contre** la vie inconnue, lui apparaissait maintenant comme **un refuge contre** la vie **trompeuse et torturante** ..."	

A "Complete" Table   103

[The borrowing continues heavily in the next paragraph.]		
p. 152	A folk tale of Nasreddin Hodja, "A l'envers sur son âne."	Bertrand makes this comparison: Annexe 4.XVIII. Nasreddin Hodja is a character in folktales from the Muslim world. See: http://nasreddinhodja.unblog.fr/2014/12/13/a-lenvers-sur-son-ane/.
"Raymond **enfourcha l'âne de son père à l'envers**, et passa au milieu des écoliers."	"Nasreddin Hodja avait **enfourché son âne à l'envers**. Les fidèles qui le suivaient lui en demandèrent la raison …"	
p. 153	Guy de Maupassant, "L'Aveugle," *Contes et nouvelles*, 1: 402–03.	Bertrand, Annexe 4.IV.
"Il allait sous le bananier de son père, la **figure toute** grisâtre, avec de **grands yeux blancs comme** du sisal battu; **et il demeurait impassible** devant les sarcasmes des galopins qui le hélaient de loin, le traitant de fainéant. **Jamais d'ailleurs** la masse des serfs n'avait salué son succès, **car aux champs**, les plumassiers de la paperasse—**sont des nuisibles, et les paysans** eussent fait **volontiers comme les poules—tuant les infirmes d'entre elles.** Quitté le Yamé, Raymond venait **s'asseoir devant la porte** de Saïf, contre le dattier de la cour. **Il ne faisait pas un geste, pas un mouvement; seules, ses paupières, qu'agitait une sorte de souffrance nerveuse, retombaient parfois** sur la tache blanche de ses yeux. Avait-il une pensée, une conscience nette de sa vie, tiraillée entre l'indigène et la française?"	"Il avait une **figure toute** pâle, et deux **grands yeux blancs comme** des pains à cacheter; **et il demeurait impassible** sous l'injure, tellement enfermé en lui-même qu'on ignorait s'il la sentait. **Jamais d'ailleurs** il n'avait connu aucune tendresse, sa mère l'ayant toujours un peu rudoyé, ne l'aimant guère; **car aux champs** les inutiles **sont des nuisibles, et les paysans feraient volontiers comme les poules qui tuent les infirmes d'entre elles.** Sitôt la soupe avalée, **il allait s'asseoir devant la porte** en été, contre la cheminée en hiver, et il ne remuait plus jusqu'au soir. **Il ne faisait pas un geste, pas un mouvement; seules ses paupières, qu'agitait une sorte de souffrance nerveuse, retombaient parfois**	

104 *Thresholds*

[Substantial borrowing continues, including almost all of the next paragraph ("Pendant ...") and the following one ("Kratonga ..."). The borrowing ends with "pour éviter les approches," p. 154.]	**sur la tache blanche de ses yeux. Avait-il un** esprit, **une pensée, une conscience nette de sa vie?** Personne ne se le demandait." [The hypotext ends on p. 404.]	
p. 155 "Han! yerago pili bara! Pourquoi qu' tu n' vas point ché les Flenèssi, avec ton Nègre-blanc au lieu de feignanter par itou? Bédéguei gombo oumo heye hein!" elle ne répondait pas, mais s'éloignait de Raymond, saisie d'une peur vague de l'inconnu, d'une angoisse de pauvre qui, brusquement, redoutait la culture de l'élève, les visages nouveaux, les Blancs, **les regards soupçonneux des gens qui ne** la **connaissaient pas;** et la vue des **gendarmes qui vont deux par deux** le long de la **route** de Krébbi-Katséna la **faisait plonger, par instinct, dans les buissons et derrière les tas de cailloux.** **Quand** elle **les apercevait au loin,** bottés, blancs et **luisants sous le soleil,** elle **retrouvait soudain une agilité singulière,** de bête, **pour gagner quelque cachette.** Elle **dégringolait** des talus, **se laissait tomber** à la façon d'une loque et se roulait en boule, devenant toute petite, invisible, rasée comme un lièvre au gite, confondant ses haillons bruns avec la terre.	Maupassant, "Le Gueux," *Contes et nouvelles,* 1:1225–26. "Il ignorait si le monde s'étendait encore loin derrière les arbres qui avaient toujours borné sa vue. Il ne se le demandait pas. Et quand les paysans, las de le rencontrer toujours au bord de leurs champs ou le long de leurs fossés, lui criaient: —Pourquoi qu' tu n' vas point dans l's autes villages, au lieu d' béquiller toujours par ci? Il ne répondait pas et s'éloignait, saisi d'une peur vague de l'inconnu, d'une peur de pauvre qui redoute confusément mille choses, les visages nouveaux, les injures, **les regards soupçonneux des gens qui ne le connaissaient pas, et les gendarmes qui vont deux par deux** sur les **routes** et qui **le faisaient plonger, par instinct, dans les buissons ou derrière les tas de cailloux.**	Orban reports from the IMEC archive that someone wrote to Seuil soon after the publication of *Le Devoir de violence,* reporting on the resemblance documented here. "Lettre de P. B. (nom réduit ici aux initiales) au Seuil, 26 mai 1969. IMEC, SEL 2923.9." See Orban, "Livre culte, livre maudit," n. 113.

"Non point qu'elle eût jamais d'affaire avec eux: mais elle portait cette terreur dans le sang, comme si elle l'eût reçu de ses parents—morts aux travaux forcés sur les chantiers des colons."	Quand il les apercevait au loin, reluisants sous le soleil, il trouvait soudain une agilité singulière, une agilité de monstre pour gagner quelque cachette. Il dégringolait de ses béquilles, se laissait tomber à la façon d'une loque, et il se roulait en boule, devenait tout petit, invisible, rasé comme un lièvre au gîte, confondant ses haillons bruns avec la terre. Il n'avait pourtant jamais eu d'affaires avec eux. Mais il portait cela dans le sang, comme s'il eût reçu cette crainte et cette ruse de ses parents qu'il n'avait point connus."	
p. 160 "Le soir tombait. Pigalle ... en procession."	Guy de Maupassant, "Le Port," *Contes et nouvelles*, 2:1125–33. The borrowings begin on p. 1126 and continue through p. 1133. This is one of the most extensive and significant sets of borrowings in the novel. They are too extensive to quote in their entirety here. See either Bertrand and Habumukiza for complete information.	See Habumukiza, 92ff. His Annexe 2 (pp. 130–41) provides a complete table of passages from "Le Port" and their corresponding passages in *DV*. See also Bertrand, Annexe 4.VII. Bertrand quotes approximately 2,800 words from *DV* (beginning with "Le soir tombait," p. 160, and ending with "jusqu'à l'aube," p. 169), flagging many of them as borrowed or paraphrastic when compared to "Le Port." More important than the copying and paraphrasing, in this case, is the plot point which Ouologuem borrows from Maupassant: a man discovers, after having sex with a prostitute, that she is his own sister. In "Le Port" the man is Célestin and the woman is Françoise; in *DV* the man is Raymond Kassoumi and the woman is Kadidia.

Borrowings from "Le Port"—which continue all the way to the top of p. 169 in *Le Devoir de violence*—are briefly interrupted on p. 161 by a borrowing from Maupassant's "Morocca." See below.

Here I will provide several examples to illustrate how Ouologuem made use of "Le Port." Words that are reproduced by Ouologuem are in bold; in this case, words that are paraphrastic are in italics.

In fact, there is a broader comparison to be made between two nineteenth-century texts that attracted Ouologuem's attention: Maupassant's "Le Port" and Flaubert's "Saint Julien." In both stories, there is a shocking revelation of a family relationship with someone who has had sex with ("Le Port") or been killed by ("Saint Julien") the protagonist. Julien kills his parents after mistaking them for his wife in bed with another man, then discovers their identity.

Textually, Ouologuem's use of "Le Port" is largely an example of "wretched paraphrase." While following the basic plot of the Maupassant, and much of the grammar, he changes many words. This is partly required by the change of context, from Marseille in the nineteenth century to Paris in the twentieth (with African protagonists). But it also shows sheer creativity on Ouologuem's part. It was not easy to do this.

Example 1: p. 160	Example 1: vol 2, p. 1126.
"*Le soir tombait.* Pigalle **s'éclairait. Dans la** *tiédeur de ce* *samedi printanier,* ils étaient *six camarades de classe* à *se mettre en* **marche, avec** une *lenteur d'êtres hésitants,* **deux par deux, en procession.**"	"La nuit était venue. Marseille **s'éclairait. Dans la** *chaleur* **de ce** *soir d'été,* un fumet de cuisine à l'ail flottait dans la cité bruyante … Dès qu'ils se sentirent sur le port, les *dix hommes que la mer roulait depuis des mois* se mirent en marche tout doucement, **avec** une hesitation d'êtres dépaysés, désaccoutumés des villes, **deux par deux, en procession.**"
	In this example, almost every word of Ouologuem is either a copy or a paraphrase of Maupassant.

A "Complete" Table   107

Example 2: p. 161	Example 2: vol. 2, p. 1127.
"Ils allaient **toujours. Partout, s'ouvraient** des *passages inconnus,* des *ruelles tortueuses, constellées d'ampoules au néon,* luisant sur le pavé gras, entre les **murs** ruisselants d'odeur **de chair de femme.**"	"**Partout, s'ouvraient** de *nouvelles rues étroites, étoilées de fanaux louches.* Ils allaient **toujours** dans *ce labyrinthe* de bouges, sur ces pavés gras où suintaient des eaux putrides, entre ces **murs** *pleins* de chair de femme."
	This example, by contrast, is very distant from plagiarism: Ouologuem has scrambled the order of things, while adhering to the general description and modernizing the context.
Example 3: p. 219	Example 3 (the moment of the revelation): vol. 2, p. 1131
"—Je le jure. —Je suis sa sœur! Il jeta son nom, *machinalement:* 'Kadidia?' Elle *l'observa* de **nouveau,** *yeux fixes,*agrandis, arrondis, **soulevés** par *une terreur horrifiée,* et elle bégaya **tout bas,** presque entre ses doigts posés sur ses lèvres: '*Quoi ... quoi?* c'est toi, Raymond?'"	"—Je le jure. —Je suis sa sœur! Il jeta son nom, *malgré lui:* —Françoise? Elle *le contempla* de **nouveau fixement,** puis, **soulevée** par une épouvante folle, par *une horreur profonde,* elle murmura **tout bas,** presque dans sa bouche: '*Oh! oh!* c'est toi Célestin?'"

108 *Thresholds*

| p. 161 | Guy de Maupassant, "Marroca," *Contes et nouvelles*, 1:371. Second use in *DV*. | Bertrand, Annexe 4.III. |

"L'orgie fut totale! Quatre mois d'économies y passèrent. Trois heures durant, exigeant une seule chambre pour mieux s'entr'exciter, ils ont fouillé, exaltés à l'excès, leurs compagnes, dont les **yeux** passés au rimmel **semblaient toujours luisants de passion;** leurs **bouches entrouvertes,** leurs **dents,** leurs **sourires même avaient quelque chose** d'étrange, **de férocement sensuel;** et leurs **seins** durs, **allongés et droits**—pointus **comme des poires de chair,** élastiques comme **s'ils eussent renfermé des ressorts d'acier**—**donnaient** à leurs caresses reflétées à l'infini par les miroirs encadrant les quatre murs capitonnés de soie, et le plafond, **quelque chose d'animal,** faisaient d'elles de superbes femelles, créatures de l'amour désordonné.

Tous les six, dans la même chambre, tantôt se regardant les uns les autres dans les miroirs, tantôt pinçant leurs compagnes, avaient **des ardeurs acharnées et des étreintes hurlantes, avec des crissements de dents, des convulsions et des morsures, suivies presque aussitôt d'assoupissements profonds comme une mort.** Mais quelqu'un éternuait ou toussotait, et tous les douze se **réveillaient brusquement,** prêts à des enlacements **nouveaux, la gorge gonflée de baisers.** Leur esprit, à

"C'était vraiment une admirable fille, d'un type un peu bestial, mais superbe. **Ses yeux semblaient toujours luisants de passion; sa bouche entr'ouverte, ses dents pointues, son sourire même** avaient quelque chose **de férocement sensuel;** et ses seins étranges, allongés et droits, aigus comme des poires de chair, élastiques comme s'ils eussent renfermé des ressorts d'acier, donnaient à son corps **quelque chose d'animal,** faisaient **d'elle une sorte d'être** inférieur et magnifique, **de créature destinée à l'amour désordonné,** éveillaient en moi l'idée des obscènes divinités antiques dont les tendresses libres s'étalaient au milieu des herbes et des feuilles.

Et jamais femme ne porta dans ses flancs de plus inapaisables désirs. **Ses ardeurs acharnées et ses hurlantes étreintes, avec des grincements de dents, des convulsions et des morsures, étaient suivies presque aussitôt d'assoupissements profonds comme une mort.** Mais elle se **réveillait brusquement** en mes bras, toute

A "Complete" Table   109

tous d'ailleurs, était simple comme un et un font deux, et un râle rauque leur **tenait lieu de pensée."** Several more phrases are borrowed, ending with "cette odeur fauve" (162)	prête à des enlacements nouveaux, la gorge gonflée de baisers. Son esprit, d'ailleurs, était simple comme deux et deux font quatre, et un rire sonore lui **tenait lieu de pensée."**	
p. 170	Guy de Maupassant, "Monsieur Parent," *Nouvelles et contes*, 2:605.	See Bertrand, Annexe 4.II.
"Il prit ainsi l'habitude de la brasserie, où le coudoiement continu des buveurs, la fumée grasse des pipes, la bière épaisse, lui alourd-issant l'esprit, calmèrent son cœur.	"Il prit ainsi l'habitude de la brasserie où le coudoiement continu des buveurs met près de vous un public familier et silencieux, où la grasse fumée des pipes endort les inquiétudes, tandis que la bière épaisse alourdit l'esprit et calme le cœur.	
Il y vécut. A peine levé, il allait chercher des voisins pour occuper son regard et sa pensée." Borrowings from this story by Maupassant continue up to "moment de la fermeture" (p. 171).	Il y vécut. A peine levé, il allait chercher là des voisins pour occuper son regard et sa pensée." The hypotext ends on p. 606.	
p. 183	Maupassant, "La Chevelure," *Contes et nouvelles*, 2:112–13.	Bertrand, Annexe 4.VIII.
"Kassoumi vit donc la mère et la fille, ses voisines de palier; il a parlé à Suzanne, **l'a tenue, l'a eue, grande, grasse, les seins** ardents, **la hanche en forme de lyre; et il a parcouru de ses caresses cette ligne ondulante et divine qui va de la gorge aux pieds en suivant toutes les courbures d'une chair** dont l'esprit, aussi simple que deux et deux font quatre, peut-être, l'accepta pour époux devant Dieu et devant les hommes."	"Les morts reviennent! Elle est venue. Oui, je l'ai vue, je **l'ai tenue,** je **l'ai eue,** telle qu'elle était vivante autrefois, **grande,** blonde, **grasse, les seins** froids, **la hanche en forme de lyre; et** j'ai **parcouru de mes caresses cette ligne ondulante et divine qui va de la gorge aux pieds en suivant toutes les courbes de la chair."**	

110   Thresholds

p. 207

"Henry: Jouez! Et changent les troubadours au Nakem l'Histoire du judaïsme. Le roi.
Saïf: **Et loué.** Jouez!"

[The phrase "Et loué" is repeated numerous times.]

p. 207 (the final paragraph of the novel):

"Souvent **il est vrai,** l'âme **veut** rêver l'écho sans passe du bonheur. **Mais,** jeté dans le monde, l'on ne **peut s'empêcher** de songer que Saïf, pleuré trois **millions de fois,** renaît sans cesse à l'Histoire, sous les cendres chaudes de plus de trente Républiques africaines …
… Ce soir, tandis qu'ils se cherchaient l'un l'autre jusqu'à ce que la terrasse fût salie des hauteurs noirâtres de l'aurore, **une** poussière chut **d'en haut sur** l'échiquier; mais à cette heure où le regard au Nakem vole autour des souvenirs, la brousse comme la côte était fébrile et brûlante de pitié. **Dans l'air,** l'eau et le feu, aussi, la terre des hommes fit **n'y avoir qu'un** jeu."

"Et loué" comes from *Le Dernier des Justes,* p. 346, the penultimate paragraph of the novel: "**Et loué.** Auschwitz. Soit. Maïdanek. L'Eternel. Treblinka. Et loué."

p. 346 (the final paragraph of the novel):

"**Parfois, il est vrai,** le cœur **veut** crever de chagrin. **Mais** souvent aussi, le soir de préférence, je **ne puis m'empêcher de penser** qu'Ernie Lévy, mort **six millions de fois,** est encore vivant, quelque part, je ne sais où … **Hier,** comme je tremblais de désespoir au milieu de la rue, cloué au sol, une goutte de pitié tomba **d'en haut sur** mon visage; mais il n'y avait nul souffle **dans l'air,** aucun nuage dans le ciel … **il n'y avait qu'un**e présence."

The final dialogue and the final paragraph of *Le Devoir* are written in imitation of the final two paragraphs of *Le Dernier des Justes.*

The fact that Ouologuem ends his novel by returning to Schwarz-Bart's novel, which thus bookends *Le Devoir,* shows the importance of this work to Ouologuem's own vision. That he copied and adapted Schwarz-Bart's final paragraph— making it his own—is a particularly audacious act of piracy, if not an open invitation to be exposed.

One notes here the heavy use of paraphrase ("souvent" instead of "parfois," "chut" instead of "tomba," etc.), along with a relatively light use of verbatim reproduction, showing the importance of adaptation for Ouologuem.

Forthcoming work by Francine Kaufmann will reveal that the final passage of *Le Devoir* quoted here is a modified version, which is then reproduced in all further reprintings of the novel. The very first printing of the novel, of September 1968, has different wording, closer to that of *Le Dernier des Justes.* Upcoming research by Kaufmann and by Jean-Pierre Orban will examine exactly how these changes were made and how extensive they were.

Index

Abraham 39
adaptation 11–13, 14, 18, 23–46, 38, 71, 84, 110
   see also Africanization; polyvocality; translation
Africanization 11, 12–13, 18, 23–27, 28, 45, 52n11
appropriation 13, 25, 29, 57–58n58
   see also borrowing
Arabic chronicles 27, 71
   Tarîkh el-Fettach 11, 19, 20, 27
   Tarîkh es-Soudan 11, 19, 20, 27
artificial intelligence 51, 65–66n130
Autret, Jean 42, 81

Baghory, George 65n120
Baldwin, James 19, 20, 21, 80–83
   Another Country 19, 20, 41, 42
Bastide, François-Régis 2, 24, 70
Bataille, Georges 52n17
Baudelaire, Charles 52n17
Bertrand, Joël 6, 7, 12, 20, 21, 51, 58n65, 67–110
   analysis of borrowings 17–18, 19, 20, 21, 56n44
Beyala, Calixthe 16
Bhabha, Homi 56n50
biblical sources 19, 20, 21, 71, 72–73, 83–84, 89–90
"blackness/authenticity" 21, 92, 96
   see also Africanization; Negritude
borrowing 2, 3, 5, 6, 9–13, 52n12

analysis of *Le Devoir de violence* 5, 6, 9–13, 50–51, 67–110
   ethics 12
   Ouologuem's defence 4
   plot devices 18
   portal of meaning 18, 27, 37, 43, 50
   summary of "complete" borrowings 67–110
   terminology 11, 13–14
   textual "collage" of sources 14–21, 23–27
   ubiquity of borrowings 10–21
   see also adaptation; copying; intertextuality; plagiarism; translation
Bouteflika, Abdelaziz 76
Brigitta, Nelly (pseudonym of Ouologuem)
   Le Secret des orchidées 2, 63n109
   Les Moissons de l'amour 3, 63n109
Burnautzki, Sarah 23, 50, 52n11
   Les Frontières de la littérature française 6
Bush, Ruth 46, 64n118
Buten, Howard 16

Camara Laye 19, 20, 21
   L'Enfant noir 15, 64n118
   Le Regard du roi 15, 17, 19, 20, 94–95
"centro verse" genre 53n21

112 *Thresholds*

Césaire, Aimé 19, 20, 21, 24, 58n63,
   91–92
   Cahier d'un retour au pays natal
     19, 20, 58n63, 74
Césaire, Suzanne 91–92
Chandler, Raymond 19, 20, 41
   The Big Sleep 19, 20, 41, 42, 95
Chaulet-Achour, Christine 5, 28–29,
   52–53n18, 69, 76, 102
collage (textual) 14, 23, 25
colonialism 14, 23–27, 29, 56n50,
   59n67, 77, 78
Constant, Paule, *White Spirit* 16
copying 13–14, 23, 25, 105
copyright ('right to copy') 13, 25, 45,
   57n57
Corbière, Edouard 74, 75
Currey, James 62n101

Decraene, Philippe 2
Delafosse, Maurice 19, 20, 26, 72–73
démarquages 11, 52n8
Diabaté, Massa Makhan 41
Diagne, Souleymane Bachir 12,
   57–58
Diakhaté, Lamine 54n30
Diallo, Adama 5
Diallo, Bakary 15
Dickinson, Emily 44, 45, 63n112,
   64n116, 96
Diop, Birago 54n30
Doubleday (publishers) 3, 50
Downs, Hugh 3

Ebodé, Eugène 6
Eliot, T. S. 44, 45, 64n116
   The Waste Land 3, 45, 64n116

Fadiman, Anne 13
falsehood 47–49
Fanon, Frantz 47, 58n63, 64n118, 74
Feuser, Wilfried F. 54n30
Flaubert, Gustave 6, 19, 20, 26,
   65–66n130, 100–01, 106

Fleming, Ian 52n17
French
   language of colonialism and power
     14, 23–27
   systemic racism of publishers 23–27
Frobenius, Leo 19, 20, 21, 24, 91–92,
   94

Galey, Matthieu 2
Garcia Márquez, Gabriel 55n35
Gary, Romain, *La Vie devant soi* 16
Greene, Graham 19, 21, 41, 45, 51n6,
   81
   It's a Battlefield 4, 10, 18, 20,
     41–43, 62n99, 84–87, 90
griot 3, 27, 71

Habumukiza, Antoine Marie Zacharie
   6, 52n17, 55n40, 69, 72, 83, 100,
   102
Hale, Thomas 58–59n66, 71
   Scribe, Griot, and Novelist 3, 27,
     71
Harcourt Brace Jovanovich (publishers)
   4, 13
Hawkins, John 74
Hérisson, Janine 42, 43, 95
Hill, Alan 4, 10, 18, 20, 41–43, 62n101
history 11–12, 26, 27–41, 50
Hitchcott, Nicki 16
hoaxes 18, 57–58
Hodja, Nasreddin 11, 19, 20, 103
Huggan, Graham 57–58n58, 92
Hugo, Victor 52n17

imitativeness ('copying/parroting') 15,
   23–24, 110
intertextuality 12, 15–17, 21, 41, 51,
   69–70, 72–73, 86–87, 102
Iphigenia 39
Isaac 39

Jeune Afrique, "Le Monde est faux" 5,
   9, 46–49, 56n44, 65n120

Jones, Ernest 64n118
Jovanovich, William 84

Kaké, Ibrahima Baba 33
Kaufmann, Francine 2, 7, 22, 50, 51, 55–56n41, 68, 110
Keïta, Chérif 7, 65n129
Kénédougou (kingdom) 29–31, 39, 41, 60n75
Kirkup, James 64n118
Konaré, Alpha Oumar 36, 60n79, 62n99
Kourouma, Ahmadou, *Les Soleils des indépendances* 25

Larson, Charles A. 64n116
The Novel in the Third World 55n40
Lautréamont, Comte de 52n17
Le Clec'h, Guy 4
Le Figaro 4
Le Monde
"Un grand roman africain" 2
"Un Nègre à part entière" 2
Leduc, Violette 18, 19, 20, 21
Thérèse et Isabelle 93
Leiris, Michel 19, 20
Afrique fantôme 74
Little, Roger 85
Lopes, Henri 16–17

Mabanckou, Alain, *Verre cassé* 17
MacDonald, John D. 19, 20, 26, 43, 81
The End of the Night 18, 26, 41, 43, 44–45, 95–100
McDonald, Robert 62–63n104
"*Bound to Violence*: A Case of Plagiarism" 4, 62–63n104
Manheim, Ralph 3, 7, 28, 44–46, 58n63, 63n115, 64n116, 74, 87, 96
Bound to Violence (English translation) 3, 7, 28, 43, 44–46, 50

Mark (evangelist) 19, 20, 83
Matthew (evangelist) 19, 20, 72
Maupassant, Guy de 2, 17, 19, 20, 26, 80, 89, 102–10
"Le Port" 18, 105–07
"Marroca" 108–09
Mazauric, Catherine 61n97
Méniaud, Jacques 36, 39–41, 59n73, 60n82, 78–79
Mensah, A. N. 45, 64n116
Messiaen, Olivier 53n19
Michel, Janine 75
Mignolo, Walter D. 24
Morrison, Captain [first name unknown] 31, 60n79–80
Mudimbe, V. Y. 56n50

NDiaye, Marie 14, 53–54n25
Ndiaye, Noémie 24
Negritude 9–10, 70, 94
New York Times 3–4

Okri, Ben, *Famished Road* 16
Olney, James 45, 64n116
Orban, Jean-Pierre 3, 7, 50, 51, 56n44, 69, 70, 95, 104, 110
Other Press (publishers) 7, 50
Ouane, Moussa, *Yambo Ouologuem: le Hogon du Yamé* 5
Ouologuem, Awa (Ava) 5, 6
Ouologuem, Yambo Amadou
accusations of borrowing from other writers 9–13, 21–22, 48
adaptive devices 23–46
author sources 17–21
borrowing from translations 41–46
constraint in writing 13–14
Le Devoir de violence 2, 9–13, 17–21, 23–46, 67–110
Le Figaro response to accusations 4, 46–49, 85
"Le Monde est faux" 5, 9, 46–49, 56n44, 65n120

114   *Thresholds*

Les Pèlerins de Capharnaüm
(unfinished) 3, 63n109
Lettre à la France nègre 3, 9, 55n37,
58n63
libel suit 4, 13
religious conversion 4, 6
withdrawal from literary scene 5–6,
10, 16, 46
writing chronology 1–7
see also Brigitta, Nelly; Rodolph,
Utto

Parinaud, André 55n41
'parroting' 15, 23–24, 110
Paul, Saint 19, 20, 89
Perec, Georges 14, 53n22
plagiarism 2, 3, 11, 21, 54n33, 73, 77,
86
Le Figaro article 4, 46–49
terminology 11, 13–14, 16, 41, 77,
86, 100–01
Pokou, Queen 39, 61n97
polyvocality 12, 18, 27–41
pornography 11, 93
portals 18, 27, 37, 43, 50
Posner, Richard A. 53n19
prélèvements 11, 52n4
Présence Africaine 1–2
Prix Goncourt 7, 14, 21–22, 25
Prix Renaudot 2, 6, 10
Proust, Marcel 52n17

racism 16, 23–27
racial profiling 23–27
Repinecz, Jonathon
Subversive Traditions 71,
72–73
Rivers, Christopher 42
Robbe-Grillet, Alain 19, 20, 87–88
Rodolph, Utto (pseudonym of
Ouologuem) 3
Les Mille et une bibles du sexe 3,
63n109, 87, 93

Rosello, Mireille 54n33
Roumain, Jacques 54n30
Roussier, Paul 19, 20, 80

sacrifice 39–41, 61n96
Sagan, Françoise, *Bonjour Tristesse*
65–66n130
Saïf (dynasty) 10, 26–27
Saleh-Dembri, Mohamed 3
sampling 25
Sano, Ba Mousso (Traoré) 39, 41,
61n96
Sanoko, Soumaïla 36
Sarr, Bacary 61n92
Sarr, Mohamed Mbougar, *La Plus*
secrète mémoire des hommes
7, 50
Schwarz-Bart, André 2, 3, 7, 12–13, 19,
20, 21–22, 50, 51n6
La Mulâtresse Solitude 22, 56n44
Le Dernier des Justes 2, 13, 17, 20,
21–22, 26–27, 69–70, 98, 110
support of Ouologuem 42, 43–44
Schwarz-Bart, Simone 22, 56n45
Sellin, Eric 3, 51n6, 69
Sembene, Ousmane 15–16
Le Docker noir 15–16, 54n30,
62–63n104
Senghor, Léopold Sédar 9–10, 24, 91,
94
Seuil (publishers) 1–2, 4, 7, 13, 22,
23–24, 25, 43–44, 65n124, 70,
85, 104
Sibon, Marcelle 42–43, 84, 90
Sikasso (siege/battle) 29–30, 31–41,
60n79, 61n96, 62n100, 76,
78–79
Slaughter, Joseph R. 45, 63n115, 94
Socé, Ousmane 65n121
Sotomayor, Sonia 57n57
Stone, Irving 19, 20
The Agony and the Ecstasy 18, 20,
75

Suret-Canale, Jean 19, 20, 21, 28–31, 37, 38–39, 59n70, 72, 76–79
  Afrique Noire Occidentale et Centrale 28–31, 76

Tansi, Sony Labou 16–17, 55n35
Tempels, Placide 92
Thomas, Dominic 15, 53–54n25, 54n30
thresholds 18, 27, 37, 43, 50
Times Literary Supplement (TLS) 10, 11, 41
  "Something *New* Out of Africa?" 4, 50, 64–65n119, 84
Touré, Samory 31, 33, 39
transformation 18, 73
Transition 4
translation 12–13, 18, 41–46, 64n118, 86
  ethical responsibility of translator 45–46
  postcolonial texts 46
Traoré, Ba Bemba 29, 31, 60n79–82
Traoré, Tiéba 31, 32, 33, 39, 40, 59n73, 61n96, 62n99

Updike, John, *Rabbit Redux* 3

Vergnaud, Lara, *The Most Secret Memory of Men* 7
Vian, Boris 42
Vigné d'Octon, Paul 19, 20, 21, 29, 31–39, 58n63, 76–78
  La Gloire du sabre 19, 20, 29, 37–39, 58n63, 59n70, 75, 76–78
violence 7, 10, 11, 31–38

Walker, Alice, *The Color Purple* 16
Walsh, Catherine E. 24
Waltraut, A. 19, 20, 21, 93
Wanberg, Kyle 92
Warhol, Andy 25, 57n57
Warner, Tobias 86
  "Bodies and Tongues" 62n102
Wise, Christopher 5, 6, 10, 52n17, 64n118, 69
Wolitz, Seth 84
Wright, Richard, *Native Son* 15–16, 54n30

Zola, Emile 52n17

Printed in the USA
CPSIA information can be obtained
at www.ICGtesting.com
CBHW070713191124
17625CB00007B/477